Bibliographies for Biblical Research

New Testament Series

in Twenty-One Volumes

General Editor

Watson E. Mills

Bibliographies for Biblical Research

New Testament Series

in Twenty-One Volumes

Volume XX

Hebrews

Compiled by

Watson E. Mills

MELLEN BIBLICAL PRESS

Lewiston/Queenston/Lampeter

Library of Congress Cataloging-in-Publication Data

Bibliographies for biblical research.

    Includes index.
    Contents: v. 20. Hebrews / compiled by
Watson E. Mills --   -- v. 20. Hebrews
    1. Bible. N.T.--Criticism, interpretation, etc.--
Bibliography.   I. Mills, Watson E.

Z7772.L1B4 1993 [BS2341.2]   016.2262'06   93-30864

ISBN 0-7734-2347-8 (v. 1) Matthew   ISBN 0-7734-2349-4 (v. 2) Mark
ISBN 0-7734-2385-0 (v. 3) Luke   ISBN 0-7734-2357-5 (v. 4) John
ISBN 0-7734-2432-6 (v. 5) Acts   ISBN 0-7734-2418-0 (v. 6) Romans
ISBN 0-7734-2419-9 (v. 7) 1 Corinthians ISBN 0-7734-2442-3 (v. 8) 2 Corinthians
ISBN 0-7734-2468-7 (v. 9) Galatians   ISBN 0-7734-2472-5 (v. 10) Ephesians
ISBN 0-7734-2474-1 (v. 11) Philippians ISBN 0-7734-2478-4 (v. 13) 1 & 2 Thessalonians
ISBN 0-7734-2480-6 (v. 14) Pastoral Epistles ISBN 0-7734-2441-5 (v. 17) 1 Peter
ISBN 0-7734-2443-1 (v. 19) 2 Peter and Jude ISBN 0-7734-2482-2 (v. 20) Hebrews
ISBN 0-7734-2438-5 (v. 21) Revelation

> This is volume 20 in the continuing series
> Bibliographies for Biblical Research
> New Testament Series
> Volume 20 ISBN 0-7734-2482-2
> Series ISBN 0-7734-9345-X

A CIP catalog record for this book is available from the British Library.

The Edwin Mellen Press   The Edwin Mellen Press
Box 450   Box 67
Lewiston, New York   Queenston, Ontario
USA 14092   CANADA L0S 1L0

Edwin Mellen Press, Ltd.
Lampeter, Dyfed, Wales
UNITED KINGDOM SA48 7DY

Printed in the United States of America

Dedication

In memory of my great great grandfather

William Breckenridge Mills

1818-1865

with great affection

Contents

Introduction to the Series

This volume is the twentieth in a series of bibliographies on the books of the Christian Bible. The series also includes volumes on the Hebrew Bible as well as the deutero-canonicals. This ambitious series calls for some 35-40 volumes over the next 3-5 years compiled by practicing scholars from various traditions.

Each author (compiler) of these volumes is working within the general framework adopted for the series, i.e., citations are to works published within the twentieth century that make important contributions to the understanding of the text and backgrounds of the various books.

Obviously the former criterion is more easily quantifiable than the latter, and it is precisely at this point that an individual compiler makes her/his specific contribution. We are not intending to be comprehensive in the sense of definitive, but where resources are available, as many listings as possible have been included.

The arrangement for the entries, in most volumes in the series, consists of three divisions: scriptural citations; subject citations; commentaries. In some cases the first two categories may duplicate each other to some degree. Multiple citations by scriptural citation are also included where relevant.

Those who utilize these volumes are invited to assist the compilers by noting textual errors as well as obvious omissions that ought to be taken into account in subsequent printings. Perfection is nowhere more elusive than in the citation of bibliographic materials. We would welcome your assistance at this point.

When the series is completed, the entire contents of all volumes (updated) will be available on CD-ROM. This option will be available, without charge, to those who have subscribed to the casebound volumes.

We hope that these bibliographies will contribute to the discussions and research going on in the field among faculty as well as students. They should serve a significant role as reference works in both research and public libraries.

I wish to thank the staff and editors of the Edwin Mellen Press, and especially Professor Herbert Richardson, for his gracious support of this series.

Watson E. Mills, Series Editor
Mercer University
Macon GA 31211
April 2000

Preface

This Bibliography on the book of Hebrews provides an index to the journal articles, essays in collected works, books and monographs and commentaries published in the twentieth century through the early months of 1999. Technical works of scholarship, from many differing traditions constitute the bulk of the citations though I have included some selected works that intend to reinterpret this research to a wider audience.

I acknowledge the work of Paul-Émile Langevin, *Bibliographie biblique* (Les Presses de l'Université Laval, 1972, 1978, 1985). This work is especially useful in verifying Catholic publications particularly citations to French literature. These volumes are meticulously indexed by scriptural citation as well as subject. Building the database necessary for a work of this magnitude was a tedious and time-consuming task. I acknowledge with gratitude the funds for travel provided by Mercer University. These funds enabled me to travel to overseas libraries during the summers of 1994, 1995, and 1998. I especially acknowledge Dean Douglas Steeples and President R. Kirby Godsey.

I want to express my gratitude to the staff librarians at the following institutions: Baptist Theological Seminary (formally of Rüschlikon, Switzerland); Oxford University (Oxford, UK); Emory University (Atlanta, GA); Duke University

(Durham, NC); University of Zürich (Zürich, Switzerland); Southern Baptist Theological Seminary (Louisville, KY) and the Richmond Theological Seminary (Richmond, VA).

Watson E. Mills
Mercer University
Macon GA 31207
April 2000

Abbreviations

AbrN	Abr-Nahrain (Louvain)
ASemB	Austin Seminary Bulletin (Austin TX)
AsiaJT	The Asia Journal of Theology (Bangalore)
ATR	Anglican Theological Review (New York)
AUSS	Andrews University Seminary Studies (Berrien Springs MI)
Bib	Biblica (Rome)
Bij	Bijdragen (Nijmegen)
BRev	Bible Review (Washington)
BSac	Bibliotheca Sacra (Dallas TX)
BT	Bible Translator (London)
BZ	Biblische Zeitschrift (Paderborn)
CBQ	Catholic Biblical Quarterly (Washington DC)
CC	Christian Century (Chicago)
CEJ	Christian Education Journal (Glen Ellyn IL)
CivCatt	La Civiltá Cattolica (Rome)
CJ	Concordia Journal (St. Louis, MO)
CJT	Canadian Journal of Theology (Toronto)
CTJ	Calvin Theological Journal (Grand Rapids MI)
CTM	Concordia Theological Monthly (St. Louis MO)
CTQ	Concordia Theological Quarterly (Fort Wayne IN)
CTR	Criswell Theological Review (Dallas)
CVia	Communio Viatorum (Prague)
Didask	Didaskalia (Lisbon)
DTT	Dansk Teologisk Tidsskrift (Cophenhagen)
EAJT	East Asia Journal of Theology (Singapore)
EB	Estudios Bíblicos (Madrid)
EE	Estudios Eclesiásticos (Madrid)
EQ	Evangelical Quarterly (London)
EstFr	Estudios franciscanos (Barcelona)

ET	Expository Times (Edinburgh)
EvT	Evangelische Theologie (Munich)
FH	Fides et Historia (Grand Rapids MI)
FilN	Filologia Neotestamentaria (Cordoba)
FirstT	First Things (New York)
FundJ	Fundamentalist Journal (Lynchburg VA)
FV	Foi et Vie (Paris)
Greg	Gregorianum (Rome)
GTJ	Grace Theological Journal (Winona Lake IN)
HTR	Harvard Theological Review (Cambridge MA)
IBS	Irish Biblical Studies (London)
Int	Interpretation (Richmond, VA)
IRM	International Review of Mission (London)
JBL	Journal of Biblical Literature (Atlanta)
JBR	Journal of Bible and Religion (Boston)
JCBRF	Journal of the Christian Brethren Research Fellowship (London)
JETS	Journal of the Evangelical Theological Society (Wheaton IL)
JMRS	Journal of Medieval and Renaissance Studies (Durham NC)
JOTT	Journal of Translation and Textlinguistics (Dallas)
JRE	Journal of Religious Ethics (Knoxville TN)
JSNT	Journal for the Study of the New Testament (Sheffield)
JTS	Journal of Theological Studies (Oxford)
Kerux	Kerux (Escondido CA)
LitJ	Liturgisches Jahrbuch (Münster)
LVie	Lumière et Vie (Lyon)
MSemJ	Master's Seminary Journal (Sun Valley CA)
MSR	Mélanges de Science Religieuse (Lille)
Neo	Neotestamentica (Pretoria)
NovT	Novum Testamentum (Leiden)
NRT	La Nouvelle revue théologique (Louvain)
NTS	New Testament Studies (Cambridge)
NTT	Norsk teologisk tidsskrift (Oslo)
OCP	Orientalia christiana periodica (Rome)
Point	Point (Papua, New Guinea)
Pres	Presbyterion (St. Louis)
RB	Revue biblique (Paris)
RechSR	Recherches de science religieuse (Paris)
RevB	Revista Biblica (Buenos Aires)
RevExp	Review and Expositor (Louisville KY)
RevQ	Revue de Qumran (Paris)
RivBib	Rivista Biblica (Brescia)
RQ	Restoration Quarterly (Austin TX)

RTP	Revue de Théologie et de Philosophie (Lusanne)
SBLSP	Society of Biblical Literature Seminar Papers (Atlanta)
SE	Sciences Ecclésiastiques (Montreal)
SJT	Scottish Journal of Theology (Edinburgh)
SkrifK	Skrif en Kerk (Pretoria)
SMT	Svensk missionstidskrift (Uppsala)
SNTU-A	Studien zum NT und seiner Umwelt (Linz)
Soj	Sojourners (Washington)
SR	Studies in Religion/Sciences religieuses (Toronto)
StTheol	Studia Theologica (Copenhagen)
StudE	Studia evangelica (Berlin)
StudPat	Studia Patristica (Berlin)
TBl	Theologische Blätter (Leipzig)
Theology	Theology (London)
TheoV	Theologische Versuche (Berlin)
ThEv	Theologia evangelica (Pretoria)
TLZ	Theologische Literaturzeitung (Leipzig)
TQ	Theologische Quartalschift (Tübingen)
TR	Theologische Rundschau (Tübingen)
TriJ	Trinity Journal (Deerfield IL)
TT	Theology Today (Notre Dame IN)
TynB	Tyndale Bulletin (Cambridge)
TZ	Theologische Zeitschrift (Basel)
VC	Vigiliae Christianae (Amsterdam)
VT	Vetus Testamentum (Leiden)
WTJ	Westminster Theological Journal (Philadelphia)
ZNW	Zeitschrift für die neutestamentliche Wissenschaft (Tübingen)
ZTK	Zeitschrift für Theologie und Kirche (Tübingen)

PART ONE

Citations by Chapter and Verse

1:1-4:13

0001 Alois Stöger, "Lebendig ist Gottes Wort: Aus Besinnungsvorträgen für Priester über Hebr 1:1-4:13," Heinz Schürmann, et al., eds., *Verbum caro factum est* (festschrift for Alois Stöger). Vienna, Austria: Niederösterreichisches Pressehaus, 1984. Pp. 12-30.

1:1-14

0002 John P. Meier, "Structure and Theology in Heb 1:1-14," *Bib* 66 (1985): 168-89.

1:1-12

0003 C. Bourgin, "Qui est Jésus-Christ?" *AsSeign* NS 10 (1970): 25-44.

1:1-6

0004 C. Bourgin, "Qui est Jésus-Christ?" *AsSeign* NS 10 (1970): 38-47.

1:1-4

0005 W. de Alfara, "El Cristocentrismo en Heb. 1,1-4," *EstFr* 60 (1959): 161-88.

1:1-4

0006 R. Schnackenburg, "Zum Offenbarungsgedanken in der Bibel," *BZ* 7 (1963): 2-13.

0007 T. Starmare, "La pienezza della Rivelazione," *BibO* 9 (1967): 145-64.

0008 Murray J. Harris, "The Translation and Significance of *Ho theos* in Hebrews 1:8-9," *TynB* 36 (1985): 129-62.

0009 Thomas G. Smothers, "A Superior Model: Hebrews 1:1-4:13," *RevExp* 82 (1985): 333-43.

0010 David Alan Black, "Hebrews 1:1-4: A Study in Discourse Analysis," *WTJ* 49 (1987): 175-94.

0011 M. J. Paul, "The Order of Melchizedek (Ps 110:4 and Heb 7:3)," *WTJ* 49 (1987): 195-211.

0012 Daniel J. Ebert, "The Chiastic Structure of the Prologue to Hebrews," *TriJ* 13 (1992): 163-79.

1:1-3

0013 D. C. Welander, "Hebrews 1:1-3," *ET* 65 (1954): 315.

0014 Ronald H. Nash, "Notion of Mediator in Alexandrian Judaism and the Epistle to the Hebrews," *WTJ* 40 (1977): 89-115.

1:1-2

0015 Albert Vanhoye, "Thema sacerdotii praeparatur in Heb. 1, 1-2,18," *VD* 47 (1969): 284-97.

0016 Mark R. Shaw, "Is There Salvation outside the Christian Faith," *EAJT* 2 (1983): 42-62.

0017 Jeffery Gibbs, "The Grace of God as the Foundation for Ethics," *CTQ* 48 (1984): 185-201.

0018 Palémon Glorieux, "La révélation du Pére," *MSR* 42 (1985): 21-41.

1:2

0019 A. M. Vitti, "Quem constituit heredern universorurn, per quern fecit et saecula," *VD* 21 (1941): 40-48, 82-87.

1:2

0020 Hugolinus Langkammer, "Den er zum Erben von allem eingesetzt hat," *BZ* NS 10 (1966): 273-80.

1:2-4

0021 S. de Ausejo, "¿Es un himno a Cristo ei prólogo du San Juan? Los himnos cristologicos de la Igiesia primitiva y el prologo del IV Evangelio," in *La escatologia individual neotestamentaria a la luz de las ideas en los tiempos apostolicos.* Madrid: Libería Científica Medinaceli, 1956. Pp. 307-96.

0022 Albert Vanhoye, "Christologia a qua initiurn sumit epistola ad Hebraeos," *VD* 43 (1965): 3-14, 49-61, 113-23.

1:3

0023 Albert Vanhoye, "De sessione caelesti in epistola ad Hebraeos," *VD* 44 (1966): 131-34.

0024 J. T. Sanders, *The New Testament Christological Hymns: Their Religious and Historical Background.* SNTSMS #15. Cambridge: University Press, 1971. Pp. 19-20, 92-94.

0025 M. A. Gourgues, "Hébreux 1:3-13," in *À adroite de Dieu.* Paris: Gabalda, 1978. Pp. 90-110.

0026   Janusz Frankowski, "Early Christian Hymns Recorded in the New Testament: A Reconsideration of the Question in the Light of Hebrews 1:3," *BZ* NS 27 (1983): 183-94.

0027   Rolf Gögler, "Inkarnationsglaube und Bibeltheologie bei Origenes," *TQ* 165 (1985): 82-94.

0028   Bernhard Heininger, "Sündenreinigung (Hebr 1,3): Christologie Anmerkungen zum Exordium des Hebräerbriefs," *BZ* NS 41 (1997): 54-68.

1:3-13

0029   Lincoln D. Hurst, "The Christology of Hebrews 1 and 2," L. D. Hurst and Nicholas T. Wright, eds., *The Glory of Christ in the New Testament: Studies in Christology.* Oxford: Clarendon Press, 1987. Pp. 151-64.

1:3-4

0030   B. Rigaux, "1 Tim 3,16; 1 P 3,18-22; 1 He 1,3-4," in *Dieu l'a ressuscité.* Gembloux: Duculot, 1973. Pp. 160-69.

1:4

0031   Jarl H. Ulrichsen, "*Diaphoroteron onoma* in Hebr 1:4: Christus als Träger des Gottesnamens," *StTheol* 38 (1984): 65-75.

1:5-10:18

0032   David Alan Black, "The Problem of the Literary Structure of Hebrews: An Evaluation and a Proposal," *GTJ* 7 (1986): 163-77.

1:5-14

0033   Albert Vanhoye, "Le Christ auprès de Dieu (Heb 1,5-14)," in *Situation du Christ: Épître aux Hébreux 1 et 2.* Paris: Cerf, 1969. Pp. 119-226.

0034   John P. Meier, "Symmetry and Theology in the Old Testament Citations of Hebrews 1:5-14," *Bib* 66 (1985): 504-33.

0035   Thomas G. Smothers, "A Superior Model: Hebrews 1:1-4:13," *RevExp* 82 (1985): 333-43.

1:5-13

0036   Paul-Gerhard Müller, "Die Funktion der Psalmzitate im Hebräerbrief," Ernst Haag and F.-L. Hossfeld, eds., *Freude an der Weisung des*

Herrn: Beiträge zur Theologie der Psalmen (festschrift for Heinrich Gross). Stuttgart: Verlag Katholisches Bibelwerk, 1986. Pp. 223-42.

0037 Herbert W. Bateman, "Two First-Century Messianic Uses of the OT: Hebrews 1:5-13 and 4QFlor 1.1-19," *JETS* 38 (1995): 11-27.

1:5-6

0038 Murray J. Harris, "The Translation and Significance of *Ho theos* in Hebrews 1:8-9," *TynB* 36 (1985): 129-62.

1:5

0039 Agustín del Agua Pérez, "Procedimientos derásicos del Sal 2:7b en el Nuevo Testamento: Tu eres mi hijo, yo te he engendrado hoy," *EB* NS 42 (1984): 391-414.

1:5

0040 Ronald Sauer, "Should the Whole Bible Be Interpreted Literally," *FundJ* 3 (1984): 32-33.

1:6-13

0041 Thomas F. Glasson, "Plurality of Divine Persons and the Quotations in Hebrews 1:6ff," *NTS* 12 (1966): 270-72.

1:6

0042 A. M. Vitti, "Et cum iterum introducit Primogenitum in orbem terme," *VD* 14 (1934): 306-12, 368-74.

0043 F. J. Schierse, "Die 'Welt' der Christus-Herrschaft," in *Verheissung und Heilsvollendung: Zur theologischen Grundfrage des Hebräerbriefes.* Münich: Zink, 1955. Pp. 93-97.

0044 Thomas F. Glasson, "Plurality of Divine Persons and the Quotations in Hebrews 1:6ff," *NTS* 12 (1966): 270-72.

0045 Antonio Vicent Cernuda, "La introducción del Primogénito, según Hebr 1:6," *EB* NS39 (1981): 107-53.

1:8

0046 Murray J. Harris, "The Translation and Significance of *Ho theos* in Hebrews 1:8-9," *TynB* 36 (1985): 129-62.

1:9

0047 I. de la Potterie, "L'onction du Christ," *NRT* 80 (1958): 225-52.

1:13-14

    0048 Murray J. Harris, "The Translation and Significance of *Ho theos* in Hebrews 1:8-9," *TynB* 36 (1985): 129-62.

1:13

    0049 M. A. Gourgues, "Hébreux 1:3-13," in *À adroite de Dieu*. Paris: Gabalda, 1978. Pp. 90-110.

1:14

    0050 William L. Lane, "Detecting Divine Wisdom in Hebrews 1:14," John H. Skilton and Curtiss A. Ladley, eds., *The New Testament Student and His Field*. The New Testament Student #5. Phillipsburg NJ: Presbyterian and Reformed Publishing Co., 1982. Pp. 150-58.

    0051 Eugene F. Klug, "The Doctrine of Man: Christian Anthropology," *CTQ* 48 (1984): 141-52.

2:1-4

    0052 Albert Vanhoye, "Situation des chrétiens," in *Situation du Christ: Épître aux Hébreux 1 et 2*. Paris: Cerf, 1969. Pp. 228-54.

    0053 Erich Grässer, "Das Heil als Wort. Exegetiscbe Erwägungen zu Hebr 2, 1-4," in H. Baltensweiler and Bo Reicke, eds., *Neues Testament und Geschichte* (festschrift Oscar Cullmann). Tübingen: Mohr, 1972. Pp. 261-74.

    0054 Thomas G. Smothers, "A Superior Model: Hebrews 1:1-4:13," *RevExp* 82 (1985): 333-43.

    0055 Alan Mugridge, "Warnings in the Epistle to the Hebrews: An Exegetical and Theological Study," *RTR* 46 (1987): 74-82.

    0056 Scot McKnight, "The Warning Passages of Hebrews: A Formal Analysis and Theological Conclusions," *TriJ* 13 (1992): 21-59.

2:1

    0057 P. Teodorico, "Metafore nautiche in Ebr. 2,1 et 6,19," *RivBib* 6 (1958): 34-49.

2:2

    0058 Ronald Williamson, "The Incarnation of the Logos in Hebrews," *ET* 95 (1983): 4-8.

2:3

0059 Gerald L. Borchert, "A Superior Book: Hebrews," *RevExp* 82 (1985): 319-22.

2:4

0060 John D. Madden, "The Authenticity of Early Definitions of Will," Felix Heinzer and Chris Schönborn, eds., *Maximus Confessor*. Fribourg: Editions Universitaires, 1982. Pp. 61-79.

2:5-3:6

0061 E. Käsemann, "Das Verhältnis von Sohn und Söhnen in Hebr. 2,5-3,6," in *Das wandernde Gottesvolk: Eine Untersuchung zum Hebräerbrief*. FRLANT #55. Göttingen: Vandenhoeck & Ruprecht, 1959. Pp. 78-105.

2:5-19

0062 Albert Vanhoye, "Le Christ auprès des hommes," in *Situation du Christ: Épître aux Hébreux 1 et 2*. Paris: Cerf, 1969. Pp. 255-387.

2:5-10

0063 F. J. Schierse, "Die zukünftige Welt des 'Menschen'," in *Verheissung und Heilsvollendung: Zur theologischen Grundfrage des Hebräerbriefes*. Münich: Zink, 1955. Pp. 97-108.

0064 Lincoln D. Hurst, "The Christology of Hebrews 1 and 2," L. D. Hurst and Nicholas T. Wright, eds., *The Glory of Christ in the New Testament: Studies in Christology*. Oxford: Clarendon Press, 1987. Pp. 151-64.

2:5-9

0065 Thomas G. Smothers, "A Superior Model: Hebrews 1:1-4:13," *RevExp* 82 (1985): 333-43.

2:5

0066 Albert Vanhoye, "L'οἰκουμένν dans l'Épître aux Hébreux," *Bib* 45 (1964): 248-53.

2:6-8

0067 P. Giles, "Son of Man in the Epistle to the Hebrews," *ET* 86 (1975): 328-32.

0068 Paul-Gerhard Müller, "Die Funktion der Psalmzitate im Hebräerbrief," Ernst Haag and F.-L. Hossfeld, eds., *Freude an der Weisung des*

Herrn: Beiträge zur Theologie der Psalmen (festschrift for Heinrich Gross). Stuttgart: Verlag Katholisches Bibelwerk, 1986. Pp. 223-42.

2:6

0069 Erich Grässer, "Beobachtungen zum Menschensohn in Hebr 2,6," in R. Pesch, et al., eds., *Jesus und der Menschensohn* (festschrift for Anton Vögtle). Freiburg: Herder, 1975. Pp. 404-14.

2:9-11

0070 Albert Vanhoye, "Destinée des hommes et chemin du Christ," *AsSeign* NS 58 (1974): 34-40.

2:9

0071 J. C. Neill, "Hebrews 2:9," *JTS* NS17 (1966): 79-82.

0072 James K. Elliot, "Jesus Apart from God," *ET* 83 (1971-1972): 339-44.

0073 James K. Elliott, "When Jesus Was Apart from God: An Examination of Hebrews 2:9," *ET* 83 (1972): 339-41.

0074 C. Samuel Storms, "Defining the Elect," *JETS* 27 (1984): 205-18.

0075 Sebastian P. Brock, "Hebrews 2:9 in Syriac Tradition," *NovT* 27 (1985): 236-44.

0076 Paul Garnet, "Hebrews 2:9: Chriti or Choris," *StudPat* 18 (1985): 321-25.

0077 F. F. Bruce, "Textual Problems in the Epistle to the Hebrews," David A. Black, ed., *Scribes and Scripture* (festschrift for J. Harold Greenlee). Winona Lake IN: Eisenbrauns, 1992. Pp. 27-39.

2:10-18

0078 Colin J. A. Hickling, "John and Hebrews: The Background of Hebrews 2:10-18," *NTS* 29 (1983): 112-16.

2:10

0079 Palémon Glorieux, "La révélation du Pére," *MSR* 42 (1985): 21-41.

0080 Julius J. Scott, "Archegos: The Salvation History of the Epistle to the Hebrews," *JETS* 29 (1986): 47-54.

0081   Alan C. Mitchell, "The Use of *prepein* and Rhetorical Propriety in Hebrews 2:10," *CBQ* 54 (1992): 681-701.

2:11

0082   J.-C. Dhotel, "La 'sanctification' du Christ d'après Hébreux 2:11," *RechSR* 47 (1959): 514-43; 48 (1960): 420-52.

2:14-15

0083   Eugene F. Klug, "The Doctrine of Man: Christian Anthropology," *CTQ* 48 (1984): 141-52.

2:14

0084   Thomas E. Schmidt, "The Letter *Tau* as the Cross: Ornament and Content in Hebrews 2,14," *Bib* 76 1 (1995): 75-84.

2:15-18

0085   D. G. Miller, "Why God Became Man: From Text to Sermon on Hebrews 2:5-18," *Int* 23 (1969): 408-24.

2:15

0086   Daniel R. Mitchell, "Man on the Eve of Destruction," *FundJ* 3 (1984): 23-27.

2:16

0087   Karl Gustav E. Dolfe, "Hebrews 2,16 under the Magnifying Glass," *ZNW* 84 (1993): 289-94.

0088   David G. Peterson, "Biblical Theology and the Argument of Hebrews," in Peterson John Pryor, eds., *In the Fullness of Time* (festschrift for Donald Robinson). Homebush West NSW: Lancer, 1992. Pp. 219-35.

2:17-18

0089   Albert Vanhoye, "Le Christ, grand-prêtre selon Héb. 2,17-18," *NRT* 91 (1969): 449-74.

3-4

0090   David Flusser, "Today If You Will Listen to This Voice: Creative Exegesis in Hebrews 3-4," Benjamin Uffenheimer, et al., eds., *Creative Biblical Exegesis: Christian and Jewish Hermeneutics through the Centuries*. Sheffield: JSOT Press, 1988. Pp. 55-62.

3:1-4:13

0091 Peter E. Enns, "Creation and Re-Creation: Psalm 95 and Its Interpretation in Hebrews 3:1-4:13," *WTJ* 55 (1993): 255-80.

3:1-6

0092 F. J. Schierse, "Das Haus Gottes," in *Verheissung und Heilsvollendung: Zur theologischen Grundfrage des Hebräerbriefes*. Münich: Zink, 1955. Pp. 108-12.

0093 Albert Vanhoye, "Grand prêtre digne de foi," in *Prêtres anciens, prêtre nouveau selon le Nouveau Testament*. Paris: Seuil, 1980. Pp. 114-19.

0094 Thomas G. Smothers, "A Superior Model: Hebrews 1:1-4:13," *RevExp* 82 (1985): 333-43.

0095 B. R. Scott, "Jesus' Superiority over Moses in Hebrews 3:1-6," *BSac* 155 (1998): 201-10.

3:2-5

0096 E. A. C. Pretorius, "Christusbeeld en Kerkmodel in die Hebreërbrief," *ThEv* 15 (1982): 3-6.

0097 Erich Grässer, "Mose und Jesus: zur Auslegung von Hebr 3:1-6," *ZNW* 75 (1984): 2-23.

3:6

0098 Gerald L. Borchert, "A Superior Book: Hebrews," *RevExp* 82 (1985): 319-22.

0099 Scott C. Layton, "Christ over His House (Hebrew 3:6) and Hebrew *'shr l-hbyt* [Gen 37-50, 1-2 Kgs]," *NTS* 37 (1991): 473-77.

0100 F. F. Bruce, "Textual Problems in the Epistle to the Hebrews," David A. Black, ed., *Scribes and Scripture* (festschrift for J. Harold Greenlee). Winona Lake IN: Eisenbrauns, 1992. Pp. 27-39.

3:7-4:13

0101 E. Käsemann, "Hebr. 3,7-4,13 als Ausgangspunkt für die Darstellung des Motives," in *Das wandernde Gottesvolk: Eine Untersuchung zum Hebräerbrief*. FRLANT #55. Göttingen: Vandenhoeck & Ruprecht, 1959. Pp. 5-8.

0102   Andrew T. Lincoln, "Sabbath, Rest, and Eschatology in the New Testament," Don A. Carson, ed., *From Sabbath to Lord's Day: A Biblical, Historical and Theological Investigation.* Grand Rapids MI: Zondervan Publishing House, 1982. Pp. 198-220.

0103   Thomas G. Smothers, "A Superior Model: Hebrews 1:1-4:13," *RevExp* 82 (1985): 333-43.

0104   Erich Grässer, "Das wandernde Gottesvolk: zum Basismotiv des Hebräerbriefes," *ZNW* 77 (1986): 160-79.

0105   Khiok-Khng Yeo, "The Meaning and Usage of the Theology of 'Rest' in Hebrews 3:7-4:13," *AsiaJT* 5 (1991): 2-33.

0106   Scot McKnight, "The Warning Passages of Hebrews: A Formal Analysis and Theological Conclusions," *TriJ* 13 (1992): 21-59.

3:7-4:11

0107   Albert Vanhoye, "Longue marche ou accès tout proche? Le contexte biblique de Hébreux 3:7-4:11," *Bib* 49 (1968): 9-26.

0108   Donald A. Hagner, "Interpreting the Epistle to the Hebrews: Hebrews 3:7-4:11," in M. A. Inch and C. H. Bullock, eds., *The Literature and Meaning of Scripture.* Grand Rapids: Baker, 1981. Pp. 217-42.

0109   Paul-Gerhard Müller, "Die Funktion der Psalmzitate im Hebräerbrief," Ernst Haag and F.-L. Hossfeld, eds., *Freude an der Weisung des Herrn: Beiträge zur Theologie der Psalmen* (festschrift for Heinrich Gross). Stuttgart: Verlag Katholisches Bibelwerk, 1986. Pp. 223-42.

3:7-4

0110   Albert Vanhoye, "Longue marche ou accès tout proche? Le contexte biblique de Hébreux 3,7-4,11," *Bib* 49 (1968): 9-26.

3:8

0111   Gerald L. Borchert, "A Superior Book: Hebrews," *RevExp* 82 (1985): 319-22.

3:11

0112   Albert Vanhoye, "Longue marche ou accès tout proche? Le contexte biblique de Hébreux 3,7-4,11," *Bib* 49 (1968): 9-26.

3:12-4:2

0113   Alan Mugridge, "Warnings in the Epistle to the Hebrews: An Exegetical and Theological Study," *RTR* 46 (1987): 74-82.

3:12-14

0114   Robert A. Peterson, "The Perseverance of the Saints: A Theological Exegesis of Four Key New Testament Passages," *Pres* 17 (1991): 95-112.

3:12

0115   Gerald L. Borchert, "A Superior Book: Hebrews," *RevExp* 82 (1985): 319-22.

3:13

0116   W. L. Lorimer, "Romans xiii. 3, Hebrews, iii. 13," *NTS* 12 (1965-1966): 389-91.

3:14

0117   Enrique Nardoni, "Partakers in Christ (Hebrews 3:14)," *NTS* 37 (1991): 456-72.

3:16

0118   E. A. C. Pretorius, "Christusbeeld en Kerkmodel in die Hebreërbrief," *ThEv* 15 (1982): 3-6.

0119   Erich Grässer, "Mose und Jesus: zur Auslegung von Hebr 3:1-6," *ZNW* 75 (1984): 2-23.

4:1-13

0120   Ann Hoch Cowdery, "Hebrews 4:1-13," *Int* 48 (1994): 282-86.

4:1-7

0121   G. Hughes, "The Son," in *Hebrews and Hermeneutics: The Epistle to the Hebrews as a New Testament Example of Biblical Interpretation.* SNTSMS #36. Cambridge: University Press, 1979. Pp. 1-31.

4:2

0122   F. F. Bruce, "Textual Problems in the Epistle to the Hebrews," David A. Black, ed., *Scribes and Scripture* (festschrift for J. Harold Greenlee). Winona Lake IN: Eisenbrauns, 1992. Pp. 27-39.

4:4-9

    0123   Roy Graham, "A Note on Hebrews 4:4-9," Kenneth A. Strand, ed., *The Sabbath in Scripture and History*. Washington: Review and Herald Publication Association, 1982. Pp. 343-45.

4:5-16

    0124   Albert Vanhoye, "Miséricorde sacerdotale," in *Prêtres anciens, prêtre nouveau selon le Nouveau Testament*. Paris: Seuil, 1980. Pp. 131-36.

4:12-13

    0125   G. W. Trompf, "The Conception of God in Hebrews 4:12-13," *StTheol* 25 (1971): 123-32.

    0126   Pierre Proulx and Luis Alonso Schökel, "Heb 4:12-13: componentes y estructura," *Bib* 54 (1973): 331-39.

    0127   Albert Vanhoye, "La parole qui juge," *AsSeign* NS 59 (1974): 36-42.

    0128   Charles M. Wood, "On Being Known," *TT* 44 (1987): 197-206.

    0129   Erich Grässer, "Hebräer 4,12-13: Etüde für einen Kommentar," Dietrich A. Koch, et al., eds., *Jesu Rede von Gott und ihre Nachgeschichte im frühen Christendum* (festschrift for Willi Marxsen). Gütersloh: Gütersloher Verlagshaus Mohn, 1989. Pp. 332-43.

    0130   Robert Van Kooten, "Guarding the Entrance to the Place of Rest: Hebrews 4:12-13," *Kerux* 11 (1996): 29-33.

4:12

    0131   H. Clavier, "*O logos tou theou* dans épître aux Hébreux," in A. J. B. Higgins, ed., *New Testament Essays* (festschrift for T. W. Manson). Manchester: University Prss, 1959. Pp. 81-93.

    0132   Palémon Glorieux, "La révélation du Pére," *MSR* 42 (1985): 21-41.

4:13

    0133   Ronald Williamson, "The Incarnation of the Logos in Hebrews," *ET* 95 (1983): 4-8.

4:14-5:10

    0134   G. Friedrich, "Das Lied vom Hohenpriester im Zusammenhang von Hebr. 4,14-5,10," *TZ* 18 (1962): 95-115.

4:14-16

0135 C. Bourgin, "La Passion du Christ et la nôtre," *AsSeign* NS 21 (1969): 15-20.

0136 Harold S. Songer, "A Superior Priesthood: Hebrews 4:14-7:27," *RevExp* 82 (1985): 345-59.

4:14

0137 K. Galling, "Durch die Himmel hindurchgeschritten," *ZNW* 43 (1950-1951): 263-64.

0138 Gerald L. Borchert, "A Superior Book: Hebrews," *RevExp* 82 (1985): 319-22.

4:15

0139 Ronald Williamson, "Hebrews 4:15 and the Sinlessness of Jesus," *ET* 86 (1974): 4-8.

4:16

0140 William Klassen, "The King as 'Living Law' with Particular Reference to Musonius Rufus," *SR* 14 (1985): 63-71.

0141 David G. Peterson, "Further Reflections on Worship in the New Testament," *RTR* 44 (1985): 34-41.

5:1-10

0142 Harold S. Songer, "A Superior Priesthood: Hebrews 4:14-7:27," *RevExp* 82 (1985): 345-59.

0143 Michael Bachmann, "Hohepriesterliches Leiden: Beobachtungen zu Heb 5:1-10," *ZNW* 78 (1987): 244-66.

5:1-6

0144 A. M. Javierre, "Réalité et transcendance du sacerdoce du Christ," *AsSeign* NS 61 (1972): 36-43.

5:1-4

0145 Albert Vanhoye, "Une description de grand prêtre," in *Prêtres anciens, prêtre nouveau selon le Nouveau Testament*. Paris: Seuil, 1980. Pp. 136-41.

5:4

0146 William Horbury, "The Aaronic Priesthood in the Epistle to the Hebrews," *JSNT* 19 (1983): 43-71.

0147 Harold S. Songer, "A Superior Priesthood: Hebrews 4:14-7:27," *RevExp* 82 (1985): 345-59.

5:5-10

0148 L. Cerfaux, "Le sacre du grand prétre, d'après Hébreux 5,5-10," *BVC* 21 (1958): 54-58.

0149 L. Cerfaux, "Die Weihe des Hohenpriesters," *BL* 26 (1958-1959): 17-21.

5:5-6

0150 Paul-Gerhard Müller, "Die Funktion der Psalmzitate im Hebräerbrief," Ernst Haag and F.-L. Hossfeld, eds., *Freude an der Weisung des Herrn: Beiträge zur Theologie der Psalmen* (festschrift for Heinrich Gross). Stuttgart: Verlag Katholisches Bibelwerk, 1986. Pp. 223-42.

5:5

0151 Agustín del Agua Pérez, "Procedimientos derásicos del Sal 2:7b en el Nuevo Testamento: Tu eres mi hijo, yo te he engendrado hoy," *EB* NS42 (1984): 391-414.

5:6-10

0152 Joseph A. Fitzmyer, "Now this Melchizedek," *CBQ* 25 (1963): 305-21.

0153 R. A. Stewart, "The Sinless High-Priest," *NTS* 14 (1967-1968): 126-35.

0154 Albert Vanhoye, "La figure de Melchisedek," in *Prêtres anciens, prêtre nouveau selon le Nouveau Testament*. Paris: Seuil, 1980. Pp. 171-93.

0155 Paul Ellingworth, "Like the Son of God: Form and Content in Hebrews 7:1-10," *Bib* 64 (1983): 255-262.

0156 Henk Jan de Jonge, "Traditie en exegese: de hogepriester-christologie en Melchizedek in Hebreeën," *NTT* 37 (1983): 1-19.

0157 Harold S. Songer, "A Superior Priesthood: Hebrews 4:14-7:27," *RevExp* 82 (1985): 345-59.

0158 Mark Kiley, "Melchisedek's Promotion to Archiereus and the Translation of *ta stoicheia tes arches*," *SBLSP* 25 (1986): 236-45.

0159   Gabriel Josipovici, "The Epistle to the Hebrews and the Catholic Epistles," in Robert Alter and Frank Kermode, eds., *The Literary Guide to the Bible*. Cambridge MA: Harvard University Press, 1987. Pp. 503-22.

0160   M. J. Paul, "The Order of Melchizedek (Ps 110:4 and Heb 7:3)," *WTJ* 49 (1987): 195-211.

0161   George H. Tavard, "The Meaning of Melchizedek for Contemporary Ministry," in Earl E. Shelp and Ronald H. Sunderland, eds., *The Pastor as Priest*. New York: Pilgrim Press, 1987. Pp. 64-85.

0162   Jerome H. Neyrey, "Without Beginning of Days or End of Life (Hebrews 7:3): Topos for a True Deity," *CBQ* 53 (1991): 439-55.

0163   Theo C. de Kruijf, "The Priest-King Melchizedek: The Reception of Gen 14,18-20 in Hebrews Mediated by Psalm 110," *Bij* 54 (1993): 393-406.

5:7-10

0164   Joachim Jeremias, "Hbr 5:7-10," *ZNW* 44 (1952): 107-11.

0165   Rueben E. Omark, "Saving of the Savior: Exegesis and Christology in Hebrews 5:7-10," *Int* 12 (1958): 39-51.

0166   Georg Braumann, "Hebrews 5:7-10," *ZNW* 51 (1960): 278-80.

0167   Martha Byskov Hansen, "Den historiske Jesus og den himmelske yppestepraest Hebraeerbrevet," *DTT* 26 (1963): 1-22.

0168   Egon Brandenburger, "Text und Vorlagen von Hebr 5:7-10: ein Beitrag zur Christologie des Hebräerbriefs," *NovT* 11 (1969): 190-224.

0169   H.-T. Wrege, "Jesusgeschichte und Jüngergeschick nach Joh 12,20-33 und Hebr. 5,7-10," in E. Lohse, et al., eds., *Der Ruf Jesu und die Antwort der Gemeinde* (festschrift for Joachim Jeremias). Göttingen: Vandenhioeck & Ruprecht, 1970. Pp. 259-88.

0170   J. Thuren, "Gebet und Gehorsam des Erniedrigten," *NovT* 13 (1971): 136-46.

5:7-9

0171   C. Bourgin, "La Passion du Christ et la nôtre," *AsSeign* NS 21 (1969): 15-20.

0172   Ortensio Da Spinetoli, "Il senso della croce nella lettera agli Ebrei: portata storica e interpretazione teologica," Christian Duquoc, et al., eds., *La sapienza della croce oggi, 1: la sapienza della croce nella rivelazione e nell'ecumenismo.* Turin: Elle Di Ci, 1976. Pp. 136-43.

5:7-8

0173   M. Rissi, "Die Menschlichkeit Jesu nach Hebr 5:7-8," *TZ* 11 (1955): 28-45.

0174   A. Feuillett, *L'agonie de Gethsémani. Enquête exégètique et théologique suivie d'une étude du 'Mystère de Jésus' de Pascal.* Paris: Gabalda, 1977.

0175   Carlos Zesati Estrada, *Hebreos 5,7-8: estudio histórico-exegéico.* Analecta Biblica #113. Rome: Pontificio Istituto Biblico, 1990.

5:7

0176   A. M. Vitti, "Exauditus est pro sua reverentia," *VD* 14 (1934): 86-92, 108-14.

0177   August Strobel, "Die Psalmengrundlage der Gethsemane-Parallele, Hebr 5:7ff," *ZNW* 45 (1954): 252-66.

0178   Emilio Rasco, "La oración sacerdotal de Cristo en la tierra segun He 5,7," *Greg* 43 (1962): 723-55.

0179   T. Boman, "Der Gebetskampf Jesu," *NTS* 10 (1963-1964): 261-73.

0180   Theodor Lescow, "Jesus in Gethsemane bei Lukas und im Hebraerbrief," *ZNW* 58 (1967): 215-39.

0181   M. Galizzi, "Ebr 5,7 e le narrazioni evangeliche," in *Gesù nel Getsemani.* Zürich: Pas, 1972. Pp. 222-40.

0182   C. Maurer, "Erhört wegen der Gottesfurcht, Hebr 5.7," in *Neues Testament und Geschichte* (festschrift Oscar Cullmann). Tübingen: Mohr, 1972. Pp. 275-84.

0183 P. Andriessen, "Angoisse de la mort dans l'épître aux Hébreux," *NRT* 96 (1974): 282-92.

5:9

0184 Edward Fudge, "The Final End of the Wicked," *JETS* 27 (1984): 325-34.

5:10-6:20

0185 Mark Kiley, "Melchisedek's Promotion to Archiereus and the Translation of *ta stoicheia tes arches*," *SBLSP* 25 (1986): 236-45.

0186 Ceslaus Spicq, "L'Epître aux Hébreux et Philon: un cas d'insertion de la littérature sacrée dans la culture profane du Iuer Psiècle," Wolfgang Haase, ed., *Principat 25, 4: Religion*. New York: Walter de Gruyter, 1987. Pp. 3602-18.

5:11-6:12

0187 Kenneth S. Wuest, "Hebrews Six in the Greek New Testament," *BSac* 119 (1962): 45-53.

0188 Scot McKnight, "The Warning Passages of Hebrews: A Formal Analysis and Theological Conclusions," *TriJ* 13 (1992): 21-59.

5:11-6:3

0189 Huw P. Owen, "The 'Stages of Ascent' in Hebrews 5:11-6:3," *NTS* 3 (1956): 243-53.

5:11-6:2

0190 E. Käsemann, "Hebr. 5,11-16,2 als Vorbereitung eines *logos teleios*," in *Das wandernde Gottesvolk: Eine Untersuchung zum Hebräerbrief*. FRLANT #55. Göttingen: Vandenhoeck & Ruprecht, 1959. Pp. 117-24.

0191 U. Wilckens, "1. Thess 1,9, 10 und Hebr 5,11-6,2," in *Die Missionsreden der Apostelgeschichte*. WMANT #5. Neukirchen-Vluyn: Neukirchener Verlag, 1974. Pp. 80-86.

5:11

0192 Gerald L. Borchert, "A Superior Book: Hebrews," *RevExp* 82 (1985): 319-22.

5:14

0193   John A. L. Lee, "Hebrews 5:14 and Exis: A History of
Misunderstanding," *NovT* 39 (1997): 151-76.

6

0194   H. Köster, "Die Auslegung der Abraham-Verheissung in Hebräer 6,"
in R. Rendtorff and K. Koch, eds., *Studien zur Theologie der
alttestainentlichen Überlieferungen* (festschrift for Gerhard von Rad).
Neukirchen-Vluyn: Neukirchener Verlag, 1961. Pp. 95-109.

6:1-8

0195   Harold S. Songer, "A Superior Priesthood: Hebrews 4:14-7:27,"
RevExp 82 (1985): 345-59.

0196   Wayne R. Kempson, "Hebrews 6:1-8," *RevExp* 91 (1994): 567-73.

6:1-6

0197   Gerald L. Borchert, "A Superior Book: Hebrews," *RevExp* 82 (1985):
319-22.

6:1

0198   P. R. P. Barker, "Studies in Texts: Hebrews 6:1f," *Theology* 65
(1962): 282-84.

0199   J. Clifford Adams, "Exegesis of Hebrews 6:1f," *NTS* 13 (1967):
378-85.

6:2

0200   Edward Fudge, "The Final End of the Wicked," *JETS* 27 (1984):
325-34.

0201   F. F. Bruce, "Textual Problems in the Epistle to the Hebrews," David
A. Black, ed., *Scribes and Scripture* (festschrift for J. Harold
Greenlee). Winona Lake IN: Eisenbrauns, 1992. Pp. 27-39.

6:4-8

0202   Herbert H. Hohenstein, "Study of Hebrews 6:4-8: The Passage in the
General Setting of the Whole Epistle," *CTM* 27 (1956): 433-44.

0203   Alan Mugridge, "Warnings in the Epistle to the Hebrews: An
Exegetical and Theological Study," *RTR* 46 (1987): 74-82.

6:4-6

0204   Charles E. Carlston, "Eschatology and Repentance in the Epistle to the Hebrews," *JBL* 78 (1959): 296-302.

0205   Philip E. Hughes, "Hebrews 6:4-6 and the Peril of Apostasy," *WTJ* 35 (1973): 137-55.

0206   Pierre Proulx and Luis Alonso Schökel, "Heb. 6.4-6: *eis metanoian anastaurountas*," *Bib* 56 (1975): 193-99.

0207   Ronald Sauer, "Can Salvation Be Lost," *FundJ* 3 (1984): 54.

6:4

0208   Peter Jensen, "Faith and Healing in Christian Theology," *Point* 11 (1982): 153-59.

6:7-8

0209   Albert Vanhoye, "Héb 6:7-8 et le mashal rabbinique," William C. Weinrich, ed., *The New Testament Age* (festschrift for Bo Reicke). 2 vols. Macon GA: Mercer Universitry Press, 1984. 1:527-32.

6:7

0210   Gerald L. Borchert, "A Superior Book: Hebrews," *RevExp* 82 (1985): 319-22.

6:9-20

0211   Harold S. Songer, "A Superior Priesthood: Hebrews 4:14-7:27," *RevExp* 82 (1985): 345-59.

6:9-11

0212   Gerald L. Borchert, "A Superior Book: Hebrews," *RevExp* 82 (1985): 319-22.

6:11-12

0213   Richard D. Patterson, "Christian Patience," *FundJ* 3 (1984): 66.

6:12-20

0214   David R. Worley, "Fleeing to Two Immutable Things, God's Oath-Taking and Oath-Witnessing: The Use of Litigant Oath in Hebrews 6:12-20," *RQ* 36 (1994): 223-36.

6:13-20

0215   Gerald L. Borchert, "A Superior Book: Hebrews," *RevExp* 82 (1985): 319-22.

6:13

0216   David G. Peterson, "Biblical Theology and the Argument of Hebrews," in Peterson John Pryor, eds., *In the Fullness of Time* (festschrift for Donald Robinson). Homebush West NSW: Lancer, 1992. Pp. 219-35.

6:18-20

0217   Marinus de Jonge, "De berichten over het scheuren van het voorhangsel bij Jezus' dood in de synoptische evangeliën," *NTT* 21 (1966): 90-114.

6:19-20

0218   Ceslaus Spicq, "*Agkyra* et *Prodromos* dans Hébr 6:19-20," *StTheol* 3 (1951): 185-87.

0219   Otfried Hofius, *Der Vorhang vor dem Thron Gottes. Eine exegetisch religionsgeschichtliche Untersuchung zu Hebräer 6,19f und 10,19f.* Tübingen: Mohr, 1972.

6:20-7:3

0220   Theo C. de Kruijf, "The Priest-King Melchizedek: The Reception of Gen 14,18-20 in Hebrews Mediated by Psalm 110," *Bij* 54 (1993): 393-406.

6:20

0221   Joseph A. Fitzmyer, "Now this Melchizedek," *CBQ* 25 (1963): 305-21.

0222   R. A. Stewart, "The Sinless High-Priest," *NTS* 14 (1967-1968): 126-35.

0223   Albert Vanhoye, "La figure de Melchisedek," in *Prêtres anciens, prêtre nouveau selon le Nouveau Testament.* Paris: Seuil, 1980. Pp. 171-93.

0224   Paul Ellingworth, "Like the Son of God: Form and Content in Hebrews 7:1-10," *Bib* 64 (1983): 255-262.

0225   Henk Jan de Jonge, "Traditie en exegese: de hogepriester-christologie en Melchizedek in Hebreeën," *NTT* 37 (1983): 1-19.

0226   Harold S. Songer, "A Superior Priesthood: Hebrews 4:14-7:27," *RevExp* 82 (1985): 345-59.

0227 Mark Kiley, "Melchisedek's Promotion to Archiereus and the Translation of *ta stoicheia tes arches*," *SBLSP* 25 (1986): 236-45.

0228 Gabriel Josipovici, "The Epistle to the Hebrews and the Catholic Epistles," in Robert Alter and Frank Kermode, eds., *The Literary Guide to the Bible*. Cambridge MA: Harvard University Press, 1987. Pp. 503-22.

0229 M. J. Paul, "The Order of Melchizedek (Ps 110:4 and Heb 7:3)," *WTJ* 49 (1987): 195-211.

0230 George H. Tavard, "The Meaning of Melchizedek for Contemporary Ministry," in Earl E. Shelp and Ronald H. Sunderland, eds., *The Pastor as Priest*. New York: Pilgrim Press, 1987. Pp. 64-85.

0231 Jerome H. Neyrey, "Without Beginning of Days or End of Life (Hebrews 7:3): Topos for a True Deity," *CBQ* 53 (1991): 439-55.

0232 Theo C. de Kruijf, "The Priest-King Melchizedek: The Reception of Gen 14,18-20 in Hebrews Mediated by Psalm 110," *Bij* 54 (1993): 393-406.

7

0233 G. T. Kennedy, "The Priesthood of Melchisedech as Found in Seventh Chapter of the Epistle to the Hebrews," in *St. Paul's Conception of the Priesthood of Melchisedech*. Washington: Catholic University of America Press, 1971. Pp. 71-107.

0234 R. Longenecker, "The Melchizedek Argument of Hebrews: A Study in the Development and Circumstantial Expression of New Testament Thought," in Robert Guelich, ed., *Unity and Diversity in New Testament Theology*. Grand Rapids: Eerdmans, 1978. Pp. 161-85.

7-13

0235 James Swetnam, "Form and Content in Hebrews 7-13," *Bib* 55 (1974): 333-48.

7-9

0236 Gerald L. Borchert, "A Superior Book: Hebrews," *RevExp* 82 (1985): 319-22.

7:1-17

0237 Joseph A. Fitzmyer, "Now this Melchizedek," *CBQ* 25 (1963): 305-21.

0238 R. A. Stewart, "The Sinless High-Priest," *NTS* 14 (1967-1968): 126-35.

0239 Albert Vanhoye, "La figure de Melchisedek," in *Prêtres anciens, prêtre nouveau selon le Nouveau Testament*. Paris: Seuil, 1980. Pp. 171-93.

0240 Paul Ellingworth, "Like the Son of God: Form and Content in Hebrews 7:1-10," *Bib* 64 (1983): 255-262.

0241 Henk Jan de Jonge, "Traditie en exegese: de hogepriester-christologie en Melchizedek in Hebreeën," *NTT* 37 (1983): 1-19.

0242 Harold S. Songer, "A Superior Priesthood: Hebrews 4:14-7:27," *RevExp* 82 (1985): 345-59.

0243 Mark Kiley, "Melchisedek's Promotion to Archiereus and the Translation of *ta stoicheia tes arches*," *SBLSP* 25 (1986): 236-45.

0244 Gabriel Josipovici, "The Epistle to the Hebrews and the Catholic Epistles," in Robert Alter and Frank Kermode, eds., *The Literary Guide to the Bible*. Cambridge MA: Harvard University Press, 1987. Pp. 503-22.

0245 M. J. Paul, "The Order of Melchizedek (Ps 110:4 and Heb 7:3)," *WTJ* 49 (1987): 195-211.

0246 George H. Tavard, "The Meaning of Melchizedek for Contemporary Ministry," in Earl E. Shelp and Ronald H. Sunderland, eds., *The Pastor as Priest*. New York: Pilgrim Press, 1987. Pp. 64-85.

0247 Jerome H. Neyrey, "Without Beginning of Days or End of Life (Hebrews 7:3): Topos for a True Deity," *CBQ* 53 (1991): 439-55.

0248 Theo C. de Kruijf, "The Priest-King Melchizedek: The Reception of Gen 14,18-20 in Hebrews Mediated by Psalm 110," *Bij* 54 (1993): 393-406.

7:1-10

0249 B. Demarest, *A History of Interpretation of Hebrews 7:1-10 from the Reformation to the Present*. Beiträge zur Geschiclite der biblischen Exegese #19. Tübingen: Mohr, 1976.

0250 Paul Ellingworth, "Like the Son of God: Form and Content in Hebrews 7:1-10," *Bib* 64 (1983): 255-262.

0251 Harold S. Songer, "A Superior Priesthood: Hebrews 4:14-7:27," *RevExp* 82 (1985): 345-59.

7:1-9

0252 David G. Peterson, "Biblical Theology and the Argument of Hebrews," in Peterson John Pryor, eds., *In the Fullness of Time* (festschrift for Donald Robinson). Homebush West NSW: Lancer, 1992. Pp. 219-35.

7:1

0253 Joseph A. Fitzmyer, "Now this Melchizedek," *CBQ* 25 (1963): 305-21.

7:3

0254 Jerome H. Neyrey, "Without Beginning of Days or End of Life (Hebrews 7:3): Topos for a True Deity," *CBQ* 53 (1991): 439-55.

0255 Mark A. Seifrid, "Paul's Approach to the Old Testament in Romans 10:6-8," *TriJ* NS6 (1985): 3-37.

7:11-19

0256 Harold S. Songer, "A Superior Priesthood: Hebrews 4:14-7:27," *RevExp* 82 (1985): 345-59.

7:11

0257 William Horbury, "The Aaronic Priesthood in the Epistle to the Hebrews," *JSNT* 19 (1983): 43-71.

0258 Harold S. Songer, "A Superior Priesthood: Hebrews 4:14-7:27," *RevExp* 82 (1985): 345-59.

7:14

0259 E. A. C. Pretorius, "Christusbeeld en Kerkmodel in die Hebreërbrief," *ThEv* 15 (1982): 3-6.

0260 Erich Grässer, "Mose und Jesus: zur Auslegung von Hebr 3:1-6," *ZNW* 75 (1984): 2-23.

7:17

    0261   Paul-Gerhard Müller, "Die Funktion der Psalmzitate im Hebräerbrief," Ernst Haag and F.-L. Hossfeld, eds., *Freude an der Weisung des Herrn: Beiträge zur Theologie der Psalmen* (festschrift for Heinrich Gross). Stuttgart: Verlag Katholisches Bibelwerk, 1986. Pp. 223-42.

7:20-28

    0262   Harold S. Songer, "A Superior Priesthood: Hebrews 4:14-7:27," *RevExp* 82 (1985): 345-59.

7:21

    0263   Paul-Gerhard Müller, "Die Funktion der Psalmzitate im Hebräerbrief," Ernst Haag and F.-L. Hossfeld, eds., *Freude an der Weisung des Herrn: Beiträge zur Theologie der Psalmen* (festschrift for Heinrich Gross). Stuttgart: Verlag Katholisches Bibelwerk, 1986. Pp. 223-42.

7:23-24

    0264   W. L. Lorimer, "Hebrews 7:23f," *NTS* 13 (1967): 386-87.

7:24

    0265   Paul Ellingworth, "The Unshakable Priesthood: Hebrews 7:24," *JSNT* 23 (1985): 125-26.

7:25

    0266   David G. Peterson, "Further Reflections on Worship in the New Testament," *RTR* 44 (1985): 34-41.

7:28

    0267   T. J. Finney, "A Proposed Reconstruction of Hebrews 7:28a in p46," *NTS* 40 (1994): 472-473.

8:1-10:18

    0268   Harold W. Attridge, "The Uses of Antithesis in Hebrews 8-10," George W. E. Nickelsburg and George W. MacRae, eds., *Christians among Jews and Gentiles* (festschrift for Krister Stendahl). Philadelphia: Fortress Press, 1986. Pp. 1-9.

8-9

    0269   Albert Vanhoye, "Thème spécifique et structure d'ensemble," in *Prêtres anciens, prêtre nouveau selon le Nouveau Testament*. Paris: Seuil, 1980. Pp. 104-99.

0270 David J. MacLeod, "The Cleansing of the True Tabernacle," *BSac* 152 (1995): 60-71.

8:1-9:10

0271 Roger L. Omanson, "A Superior Covenant: Hebrews 8:1-10:18," *RevExp* 82 (1985): 361-73.

8:1-6

0272 David G. Peterson, "Further Reflections on Worship in the New Testament," *RTR* 44 (1985): 34-41.

8:3-9:10

0273 Albert Vanhoye, "La critique du culte ancien." in *Prêtres anciens, prêtre nouveau selon le Nouveau Testament*. Paris: Seuil, 1980. Pp. 199-212.

8:5

0274 E. A. C. Pretorius, "Christusbeeld en Kerkmodel in die Hebreërbrief," *ThEv* 15 (1982): 3-6.

0275 Lincoln D. Hurst, "How 'Platonic' Are Hebrews 8:5 and Hebrews 9:23f?" *JTS* NS34 (1983): 156-68.

0276 Erich Grässer, "Mose und Jesus: zur Auslegung von Hebr 3:1-6," *ZNW* 75 (1984): 2-23.

0277 Hermut Löhr, " 'Umriss' und 'Schatten': Bemerkungen zur Zitierung von Ex 25,40 in Hebr 8," *ZNW* 84 (1993): 218-32.

8:8

0278 Johannes L. P. Wolmarans, "The Text and Translation of Hebrews 8:8," *ZNW* 75 (1984): 139-44.

8:11

0279 Otfried Hofius, *Katapausis: Die Vorstellung vom endzeitlichen Ruheort im Hebräerbrief*. WUNT #11. Tübingen: Mohr, 1970.

8:18

0280 Otfried Hofius, *Katapausis: Die Vorstellung vom endzeitlichen Ruheort im Hebräerbrief*. WUNT #11. Tübingen: Mohr, 1970.

9-10

0281   Gary S. Selby, "The Meaning and Function of *syneidesis* in Hebrews
9 and 10," *RQ* 28 (1986): 145-54.

9

0282   Irena Backus, "Piscator Misconstrued: Some Remarks on Robert
Rollock's 'Logical Analysis' of Hebrews 9," *JMRS* 14 (1984):
113-19.

0283   Pierre Fraenkel, "Matthias Flacius Illyricus and his Gloss on Hebrews
9," *JMRS* 14 (1984): 97-111.

0284   Henk Jan de Jonge, "The Character of Erasmus' Translation of the
New Testament as Reflected in His Translation of Hebrews 9," *JMRS*
14 (1984): 81-87.

0285   Luc Perrottet, "Chapter 9 of the Epistle to the Hebrews as Presented
in an Unpublished Course of Lectures by Theodore Beza," *JMRS* 14
(1984): 89-96.

0286   Marcel Tetel, "Text, Translation, and Exegesis of Hebrews 9," *JMRS*
14 (1984): 77-119.

9:1-17

0287   Wilhelm Thüsing, "Lasst uns hinzutreten (Hebr 10:22): zur Frage nach
dem Sinn der Kulttheologie im Hebräerbrief," *BZ* NS9 (1965): 1-17.

9:1-14

0288   Paul Ellingworth, "Jesus and the Universe in Hebrews," *EQ* 58
(1986): 337-350.

9:1-10

0289   Otfried Hofius, "Das 'erste' und das 'zweite' Zelt, ein Beitrag zur
Auslegung von Hbr 9,1-10," *ZNW* 61 (1970): 271-77.

9:2-5

0290   Sever J. Voicu, "Gennadio di Costantinopoli: La trasmissione del
frammento In Hebr 9,2-5," *OCP* 48 (1982): 435-37.

9:2

0291   L. Sabourin, "Liturge du Sanctuaire et de la Tente Véritable," *NTS* 18
(1971-1972): 87-90.

9:3-4

0292   Harold S. Camacho, "The Altar of Incense in Hebrews 9:3-4," *AUSS* 24 (1986): 5-12.

9:4-5

0293   Olaf Moe, "Das irdische und das himmlische Heiligtum: Zur Auslegung von Hebr 9:4f," *TZ* 9 (1953): 23-29.

9:4

0294   William Horbury, "The Aaronic Priesthood in the Epistle to the Hebrews," *JSNT* 19 (1983): 43-71.

0295   Harold S. Songer, "A Superior Priesthood: Hebrews 4:14-7:27," *RevExp* 82 (1985): 345-59.

9:6-10

0296   Steve Stanley, "Hebrews 9:6-10: The 'Parable' of the Tabernacle," *NovT* 37 (1995): 385-99.

9:9-10

0297   James Swetnam, "On the Imagery and Significance of Hebrews 9:9-10," *CBQ* 28 (1966): 155-73.

0298   Nello Casalini, "I sacrifici dell'antica alleanza nel piano salvifico di Dio secondo la lettera agli Ebrei," *RivBib* 35 (1987): 443-64.

9:9

0299   Gerald L. Borchert, "A Superior Book: Hebrews," *RevExp* 82 (1985): 319-22.

9:10-23

0300   John Murray, "Christian Baptism," *WTJ* 13 (1951): 105-50.

9:11-28

0301   Roger L. Omanson, "A Superior Covenant: Hebrews 8:1-10:18," *RevExp* 82 (1985): 361-73.

9:11-15

0302   C. Bourgin, " La notivelle alliance dans le sang du Christ," *AsSeign* NS 32 (1971): 40-45.

9:11

0303   Jose M. Bover, "Las variante mellonton y genomenon en Hebrews 9:11," *Bib* 32 (1951): 232-36.

0304   Albert Vanhoye, "Par la tente plus grande et plus parfaite (He 9:11)," *Bib* 46 (1965): 1-28.

0305   James Swetnam, "Greater and More Perfect Tent: A Contribution to the Discussion of Hebrews 9:11," *Bib* 47 (1966): 91-106.

0306   P. Andriessen, "Das grössere und vollkornmenere Zelt," *BZ* 15 (1971): 76-92.

0307   F. F. Bruce, "Textual Problems in the Epistle to the Hebrews," David A. Black, ed., *Scribes and Scripture* (festschrift for J. Harold Greenlee). Winona Lake IN: Eisenbrauns, 1992. Pp. 27-39.

9:12

0308   Edward Fudge, "The Final End of the Wicked," *JETS* 27 (1984): 325-34.

0309   Franz Laub, "Ein für allemal hineingegangen in das Allerheiligste (Hebr 9:12)--zum Verständnis des Kreuzestodes im Hebräerbrief," *BZ* NS35 (1991): 65-85.

9:14

0310   Albert Vanhoye, "Esprit éternel et feu du sacrifice en He 9:14," *Bib* 64 (1983): 263-274.

9:15-18

0311   James Swetnam, "Suggested Interpretation of Hebrews 9:15-18," *CBQ* 27 (1965): 373-90.

9:15-16

0312   W. Selb, "*Diathēkē* im Neuen Testament," in B. S. Jackson, ed., *Studies in Jewish Legal History* (festschrift for David Daube). London: Jewish Chronicle Puiblicatins, 1974. Pp. 183-96.

9:16-17

0313   K. M. Campbell, "Covenant or Testament? Hebrews 9:16,17 Reconsidered," *EQ* 44 (1972): 107-111.

9:19

0314 E. A. C. Pretorius, "Christusbeeld en Kerkmodel in die Hebreërbrief," *ThEv* 15 (1982): 3-6.

0315 Erich Grässer, "Mose und Jesus: zur Auslegung von Hebr 3:1-6," *ZNW* 75 (1984): 2-23.

0316 F. F. Bruce, "Textual Problems in the Epistle to the Hebrews," David A. Black, ed., *Scribes and Scripture* (festschrift for J. Harold Greenlee). Winona Lake IN: Eisenbrauns, 1992. Pp. 27-39.

9:22

0317 T. C. G. Thornton, "Meaning of *ahimatekchysia* in Hebrews 9:22," *JTS* NS15 (1964): 63-65.

9:23

0318 Lincoln D. Hurst, "How 'Platonic' Are Hebrews 8:5 and Hebrews 9:23f?" *JTS* NS34 (1983): 156-68.

9:24-28

0319 Albert Vanhoye, "L'intervention décisive du Christ," *AsSeign* NS 63 (1971): 47-52.

9:24

0320 C. T. Fritsch, "*To antitupon*," in *Studia Biblica et Semitica*. Wageningen: Veenman & Zonen, 1966. Pp. 100-107.

10-13

0321 Mark L. Sargent, "Strangers on the Earth: William Bradford, The Epistle to the Hebrews and the Plymouth 'Pilgrims'," *FH* 24 (1992): 18-41.

10

0322 Albert Vanhoye, "Un sacrifice efficace," in *Prêtres anciens, prêtre nouveau selon le Nouveau Testament*. Paris: Seuil, 1980. Pp. 236-63.

0323 August Konkel, "The Sacrifice of Obedience," *Didask* 2 (1991): 2-11.

10:1-18

0324 Roger L. Omanson, "A Superior Covenant: Hebrews 8:1-10:18," *RevExp* 82 (1985): 361-73.

10:1-4

0325 Nello Casalini, "I sacrifici dell'antica alleanza nel piano salvifico di Dio secondo la lettera agli Ebrei," *RivBib* 35 (1987): 443-64.

10:1

0326 F. F. Bruce, "A Shadow of Good Things to Come," in *The Time is Fulfilled: Five Aspects of the Fulfilment of the Old Testament in the New*. Exeter: Paternoster, 1978. Pp. 75-94.

0327 David G. Peterson, "Further Reflections on Worship in the New Testament," *RTR* 44 (1985): 34-41.

0328 F. F. Bruce, "Textual Problems in the Epistle to the Hebrews," David A. Black, ed., *Scribes and Scripture* (festschrift for J. Harold Greenlee). Winona Lake IN: Eisenbrauns, 1992. Pp. 27-39.

10:5-10

0329 P. Andriessen, "Le seul sacrifice qui plait à Dieu," *AsSeign* NS 8 (1972): 58-63.

0330 Armando J. Levoratti, "Tú no has querido sacrificio ni oblación: Salmo 40:7; Hebreos 10:5; pt 2," *RevB* 48 (1986): 193-237.

0331 Paul-Gerhard Müller, "Die Funktion der Psalmzitate im Hebräerbrief," Ernst Haag and F.-L. Hossfeld, eds., *Freude an der Weisung des Herrn: Beiträge zur Theologie der Psalmen* (festschrift for Heinrich Gross). Stuttgart: Verlag Katholisches Bibelwerk, 1986. Pp. 223-42.

10:5-7

0332 Karen H. Jobes, "The Function of *paronomasia* in Hebrews 10:5-7," *TriJ* 13 (1992): 181-91.

10:5

0333 Albert Brandenburg, "Solae aures sunt organa Christiani hominis (Luther) Zu Luthers Exegese von Hebr 10, 5f," Joseph Ratzinger and Heinrich Fries, eds., *Einsicht und Glaube* (festschrift for Gottlieb Söhngen). Freiburg: Herder, 1962. Pp. 401-404.

10:12

0334 M. A. Gourgues, "Hébreux 8:1 et 10:12," in *À adroite de Dieu*. Paris: Gabalda, 1978. Pp. 110-19.

10:19-13:17

0335 David Alan Black, "The Problem of the Literary Structure of Hebrews: An Evaluation and a Proposal," *GTJ* 7 (1986): 163-77.

10:19-39

0336 R. Alan Culpepper, "A Superior Faith: Hebrews 10:19-12:2," *RevExp* 82 (1985): 375-90.

0337 Scot McKnight, "The Warning Passages of Hebrews: A Formal Analysis and Theological Conclusions," *TriJ* 13 (1992): 21-59.

10:19-25

0338 Nils A. Dahl, "A New and Living Way: The Approach to God according to Hebrews 10:19-25," *Int* 5 (1951): 401-12.

0339 F. J. Schierse, "Der Priesterdienst der Gemeinde am himmlischen Heiligtum," in *Verheissung und Heilsvollendung: Zur theologischen Grundfrage des Hebräerbriefes.* Münich: Zink, 1955. Pp. 166-71.

0340 Otto Glombitza, "Erwägungen zum kunstvollen Ansatz der Paraenese im Brief an die Hebräer 10:19-25," *NovT* 9 (1967): 132-50.

10:19-20

0341 Otfried Hofius, "Inkarnation und Opfertod Jesu nach Hebr 10, 19. f.," in *Der Ruf Jesu und die Antwort der Gemeinde* (festschrift for Joachim Jeremias). Göttingen: Vandenhioeck & Ruprecht, 1970. Pp. 132-41.

10:19

0342 Otfried Hofius, *Der Vorhang vor dem Thron Gottes. Eine exegetisch religionsgeschichtliche Untersuchung zu Hebräer 6,19f und 10,19f.* Tübingen: Mohr, 1972.

10:20

0343 Joachim Jeremias, "Hebrér 10:20: tout' estin tes sarkos autou," *ZNW* 62 (1971): 131.

0344 Norman H. Young, "*Tout' estin tes sarkos autou*: Apposition, Dependent or Explicative?" *NTS* 20 (1973): 100-104.

10:21

0345 F. J. Schierse, "Das Haus Gottes," in *Verheissung und Heilsvollendung: Zur theologischen Grundfrage des Hebräerbriefes.* München: Zink, 1955. Pp. 108-12.

10:22

0346 David G. Peterson, "Further Reflections on Worship in the New Testament," *RTR* 44 (1985): 34-41.

10:26-31

0347 Alan Mugridge, "Warnings in the Epistle to the Hebrews: An Exegetical and Theological Study," *RTR* 46 (1987): 74-82.

10:26-29

0348 Charles E. Carlston, "Eschatology and Repentance in the Epistle to the Hebrews," *JBL* 78 (1959): 296-302.

10:28

0349 E. A. C. Pretorius, "Christusbeeld en Kerkmodel in die Hebreërbrief," *ThEv* 15 (1982): 3-6.

0350 Erich Grässer, "Mose und Jesus: zur Auslegung von Hebr 3:1-6," *ZNW* 75 (1984): 2-23.

10:30-31

0351 James Swetnam, "Hebrews 10,30-31: A Suggestion," *Bib* 75 (1994): 388-94.

10:32-13:17

0352 D. Kim, "Perseverance in Hebrews," *SkrifK* 18 (1997): 280-90.

10:32-39

0353 Richard D. Patterson, "Christian Patience," *FundJ* 3 (1984): 66.

10:33

0354 H. J. Cadbury, "*Theatrizō* No Longer a New Testament *hapax legomenon*," *ZNW* 29 (1930): 60-63.

10:37-38

0355 J. Duncan M. Derrett, "Running in Paul: The Midrashic Potential of Habakkuk 2:2," *Bib* 66 (1985): 560-67.

10:38

0356 F. F. Bruce, "Textual Problems in the Epistle to the Hebrews," David A. Black, ed., *Scribes and Scripture* (festschrift for J. Harold Greenlee). Winona Lake IN: Eisenbrauns, 1992. Pp. 27-39.

11-13

0357 Harold S. Songer, "A Superior Priesthood: Hebrews 4:14-7:27," *RevExp* 82 (1985): 345-59.

0358 Alan Mugridge, "Warnings in the Epistle to the Hebrews: An Exegetical and Theological Study," *RTR* 46 (1987): 74-82.

11-12

0359 Stanley Frost, "Who Were the Heroes: An Exercise in Bi-testamentary Exegesis, with Christological Implications L. D. Hurst and Nicholas T. Wright, eds., *The Glory of Christ in the New Testament: Studies in Christology.* Oxford: Clarendon Press, 1987. Pp. 165-72.

11:1-12:2

0360 Merland Ray Miller, "What is the Literary Form of Hebrews 11," *JETS* 29 (1986): 419-27.

11

0361 Gottfried Schille, "Katechese und Taufliturgie: Erwägungen zu Hbr 11," *ZNW* 51 (1960): 112-31.

0362 F. Bovon, "Le Christ, la foi et la sagesse dans l'épître aux Hébreux," *RTP* 18 (1968): 129-44.

0363 Gerald L. Borchert, "A Superior Book: Hebrews," *RevExp* 82 (1985): 319-22.

0364 Chris Michael, "Glimpses of the Kingdom in the Urban Church," Donald B. Rogers, ed., *Urban Church Education.* Birmingham: Religious Education Press, 1989. Pp. 41-49.

0365 Kimberly F. Baker, "Hebrews 11--The Promise of Faith," *RevExp* 94 (1997): 439-45.

0366 Pamela M. Eisenbaum, *The Jewish Heroes of Christian History: Hebrews 11 in Literary Context.* DSSBL # 156. Atlanta: Scholars Press, 1997.

0367   V. Rhee, "Chiasm and the Concept of Faith in Hebrews 11," *BSac* 155
(1998): 327-45.

11:1-3

0368   R. Alan Culpepper, "A Superior Faith: Hebrews 10:19-12:2," *RevExp*
82 (1985): 375-90.

0369   Richard A. Spencer, "Hebrews 11:1-3, 8-16," *Int* 49 (1995): 288-92.

11:1

0370   Heinrich Dörrie, "Zu Hbr 11:1," *ZNW* 46 (1955): 196-202.

0371   Klaus Haacker, "Der Glaube im Hebräerbrief und die hermeneutische
Bedeutung des Holocaust," *TZ* 39 (1983): 152-65.

0372   Luis F. Ladaria, "Presente y futuro en la escatología cristiana," *EE* 60
(1985): 351-59.

0373   Otto Betz, "Firmness in faith: Hebrews 11:1 and Isaiah 28:16," in
Barry P. Thompson, ed., *Scripture: Meaning and Method* (festschrift
for A. T. Hanson). Hull UK: Hull University Press, 1987. Pp. 92-113.

0374   Robert G. Hoerber, "On the Translation of Hebrews 11:1," *CJ* 21
(1995): 77-79.

0375   E. Mengelle, "La estructura de Hebreos 11, 1," *Bib* 78 (1997):
534-42.

11:3

0376   Klaus Haacker, "Creatio ex auditu: zum Verstandnis von Hbr 11:3,"
ZNW 60 (1969): 279-81.

11:4-7

0377   R. Alan Culpepper, "A Superior Faith: Hebrews 10:19-12:2," *RevExp*
82 (1985): 375-90.

11:5

0378   J. H. Greenlee, "A Question of Tenses: Hebrews 11:15," *NTrans* 11
(1997): 52-56.

11:6

0379   David G. Peterson, "Further Reflections on Worship in the New
Testament," *RTR* 44 (1985): 34-41.

11:7

0380 Bernhard Heininger, "Hebr 11.7 unddas Henochorakel am Ende der Welt," *NTS* 44 (1998): 115-32.

11:8-16

0381 Richard A. Spencer, "Hebrews 11:1-3, 8-16," *Int* 49 (1995): 288-92.

11:8-12

0382 R. Alan Culpepper, "A Superior Faith: Hebrews 10:19-12:2," *RevExp* 82 (1985): 375-90.

11:8-10

0383 L. M. Muntingh, " 'The City which Has Foundations': Hebrews 11:8-10 in the Light of the Mari Texts," in I. H. Eybers, et al., eds., *De Fructu Ons Sui* (festschrift for Adrianus van Sels). Leiden: Brill, 1971. Pp. 108-20.

11:8

0384 George Duncan, "Obedience and Faith," David Porter, ed., *The People and the King*. Bromley, England: Send the Light Trust, 1980. Pp. 122-27.

0385 David G. Peterson, "Biblical Theology and the Argument of Hebrews," in Peterson John Pryor, eds., *In the Fullness of Time* (festschrift for Donald Robinson). Homebush West NSW: Lancer, 1992. Pp. 219-35.

11:10-16

0386 F. J. Schierse, "Das Vaterland - eine Himmelsstadt," in *Verheissung und Heilsvollendung: Zur theologischen Grundfrage des Hebräerbriefes*. München: Zink, 1955. Pp. 121-26.

11:11

0387 M. Black, "Critical and Exegetical notes on Three New Testament Texts: Hebrews xi. 11, Jude 5, James i. 2,7," in *Apophoreta* (festschrift for Ernst Haencehn). BZNW #30. Berlin: Töpelmann, 1964. Pp. 39-45.

0388 F. F. Bruce, "Textual Problems in the Epistle to the Hebrews," David A. Black, ed., *Scribes and Scripture* (festschrift for J. Harold Greenlee). Winona Lake IN: Eisenbrauns, 1992. Pp. 27-39.

0389   Pieter W. van der Horst, "Did Sarah Have a Seminal Emission?" *BRev* 8 (1992): 35-39.

11:13-16
0390   R. Alan Culpepper, "A Superior Faith: Hebrews 10:19-12:2," *RevExp* 82 (1985): 375-90.

11:14
0391   F. J. Schierse, "Das himmlische Vaterland," in *Verheissung und Heilsvollendung: Zur theologischen Grundfrage des Hebräerbriefes.* München: Zink, 1955. Pp. 115-21.

11:17-22
0392   R. Alan Culpepper, "A Superior Faith: Hebrews 10:19-12:2," *RevExp* 82 (1985): 375-90.

11:17-19
0393   James Swetnam, *Jesus and Isaac: A Study of the Epistle to the Hebrews in the Light of the Aqedah.* Analecta Biblica #94. Rome: Biblical Institute Press, 1981.

11:21
0394   Moisés Silva, "The New Testament Use of the Old Testament: Text Form and Authority," Don A. Carson and John D. Woodbridge, eds., *Scripture and Truth.* Grand Rapids: Zondervan, 1983. Pp. 147-65.

11:23-28
0395   R. Alan Culpepper, "A Superior Faith: Hebrews 10:19-12:2," *RevExp* 82 (1985): 375-90.

11:23-24
0396   E. A. C. Pretorius, "Christusbeeld en Kerkmodel in die Hebreërbrief," *ThEv* 15 (1982): 3-6.

0397   Erich Grässer, "Mose und Jesus: zur Auslegung von Hebr 3:1-6," *ZNW* 75 (1984): 2-23.

11:24-28
0398   A. T. Hanson, "The Reproach of the Messiah in the Epistle to the Hebrews," in *StudE* 7 (1982): 231-40.

11:29-31

0399 R. Alan Culpepper, "A Superior Faith: Hebrews 10:19-12:2," *RevExp* 82 (1985): 375-90.

11:31

0400 William H. Willimon, "Best Little Harlot's House in Jericho," *CC* 100 (1983): 956-58.

11:32-12:2

0401 Murphy Davis, "Turning Dreams into Deeds: Faith in the Unseen Realities," *Soj* 14 (1985): 21-22.

11:32-38

0402 R. Alan Culpepper, "A Superior Faith: Hebrews 10:19-12:2," *RevExp* 82 (1985): 375-90.

11:33-38

0403 Michel van Esbroeck, "Hébreux 11:33-38 dans l'ancienne version géorgienne," *Bib* 53 (1972): 43-64.

11:37

0404 F. F. Bruce, "Textual Problems in the Epistle to the Hebrews," David A. Black, ed., *Scribes and Scripture* (festschrift for J. Harold Greenlee). Winona Lake IN: Eisenbrauns, 1992. Pp. 27-39.

11:39-40

0405 R. Alan Culpepper, "A Superior Faith: Hebrews 10:19-12:2," *RevExp* 82 (1985): 375-90.

12:1-29

0406 Scot McKnight, "The Warning Passages of Hebrews: A Formal Analysis and Theological Conclusions," *TriJ* 13 (1992): 21-59.

12:1-13

0407 N. Clayton Croy, *Endurance in Suffering: Hebrews 12:1-13 in Its Rhetorical, Religious, and Philosophical Context.* Cambridge: University Press, 1998.

12:1-3

0408 Harold L. Willmington, "Jesus Christ: The Misunderstood," *FundJ* 2 (1983): 42.

0409 Gerald L. Borchert, "A Superior Book: Hebrews," *RevExp* 82 (1985): 319-22.

12:1-2

0410 Klaus Haacker, "Der Glaube im Hebräerbrief und die hermeneutische Bedeutung des Holocaust," *TZ* 39 (1983): 152-65.

0411 Harold L. Willmington, "God's Super Bowl," *FundJ* 3 (1984): 49.

0412 R. Alan Culpepper, "A Superior Faith: Hebrews 10:19-12:2," *RevExp* 82 (1985): 375-90.

0413 David Alan Black, "A Note on the Structure of Hebrews 12:1-2," *Bib* 68 (1987): 543-51.

12:1

0414 Alberto Vaccari, "Hebr 12,1: lectio emendatior," *Bib* 39 (1958): 471-77.

0415 J. D. Robb, "Hebrews 12:1," *ET* 79 (1968): 254.

0416 F. F. Bruce, "Textual Problems in the Epistle to the Hebrews," David A. Black, ed., *Scribes and Scripture* (festschrift for J. Harold Greenlee). Winona Lake IN: Eisenbrauns, 1992. Pp. 27-39.

12:2

0417 Julius J. Scott, "Archegos: The Salvation History of the Epistle to the Hebrews," *JETS* 29 (1986): 47-54.

0418 N. Clayton Croy, "A Note on Hebrews 12:2," *JBL* 114 (1995): 117-119.

12:3

0419 F. F. Bruce, "Textual Problems in the Epistle to the Hebrews," David A. Black, ed., *Scribes and Scripture* (festschrift for J. Harold Greenlee). Winona Lake IN: Eisenbrauns, 1992. Pp. 27-39.

12:3-11

0420 Peter R. Jones, "A Superior Life: Hebrews 12:3-13:25," *RevExp* 82 (1985): 391-405.

12:4-17

0421 Bill Kellermann, "The Curse and Blessing of the Wilderness: The Risky Inheritance of Hebrews," *Soj* 14 (1985): 24-27.

12:12-17
0422 Gerald L. Borchert, "A Superior Book: Hebrews," *RevExp* 82 (1985): 319-22.

0423 Peter R. Jones, "A Superior Life: Hebrews 12:3-13:25," *RevExp* 82 (1985): 391-405.

0424 Alan Mugridge, "Warnings in the Epistle to the Hebrews: An Exegetical and Theological Study," *RTR* 46 (1987): 74-82.

12:14-17
0425 Robert A. Peterson, "The Perseverance of the Saints: A Theological Exegesis of Four Key New Testament Passages," *Pres* 17 (1991): 95-112.

12:17
0426 Charles E. Carlston, "Eschatology and Repentance in the Epistle to the Hebrews," *JBL* 78 (1959): 296-302.

0427 R. Talbot Watkins, "New English Bible and the Translation of Hebrews 12:17," *ET* 73 (1961): 29-30.

12:18-29
0428 F. J. Schierse, "Gericht und Danksagung," in *Verheissung und Heilsvollendung: Zur theologischen Grundfrage des Hebräerbriefes.* Münich: Zink, 1955. Pp. 171-84.

0429 William Klassen, "To the Hebrews or against the Hebrews: Anti-Judaism and the Epistle to the Hebrews," Stephen Wilson, ed., *Anti-Judaism in Early Christianity.* Volume 2: *Separation and Polemic.* Studies in Christianity and Judaism #2. Waterloo, Ontario: Wilfried Laurier University Press, 1986. Pp. 1-16.

12:18-24
0430 B. Gartner, *The Temple and the Community in Qumran and the New Testament.* Cambridge: University Press, 1965. Pp. 88-99.

0431 Tomasz Jelonek, "Palpabile et 'Mons Sion': de vero sensu antithesis in Hbr 12,18-24," Adam Kubis, et al., *Analecta Cracoviensia, 1977.* Krakow: Polskie Towarzystwo Teologiczne, 1977. Pp. 139-54.

0432 Peter R. Jones, "A Superior Life: Hebrews 12:3-13:25," *RevExp* 82 (1985): 391-405.

12:18

0433   David G. Peterson, "Further Reflections on Worship in the New Testament," *RTR* 44 (1985): 34-41.

12:21

0434   Jan Heller, "Stabesanbetung?" *CVia* 16 (1973): 257-65.

0435   E. A. C. Pretorius, "Christusbeeld en Kerkmodel in die Hebreërbrief," *ThEv* 15 (1982): 3-6.

0436   Erich Grässer, "Mose und Jesus: zur Auslegung von Hebr 3:1-6," *ZNW* 75 (1984): 2-23.

12:22

0437   Ceslaus Spicq, "La Panégyrie de Hebr 12:22," *StTheol* 6 (1952): 30-38.

0438   David G. Peterson, "Further Reflections on Worship in the New Testament," *RTR* 44 (1985): 34-41.

12:23

0439   Charles R. Smith, "The Book of Life," *GTJ* 6 (1985): 219-30.

12:25-29

0440   Peter R. Jones, "A Superior Life: Hebrews 12:3-13:25," *RevExp* 82 (1985): 391-405.

0441   Alan Mugridge, "Warnings in the Epistle to the Hebrews: An Exegetical and Theological Study," *RTR* 46 (1987): 74-82.

12:25-28

0442   Erich Grässer, "Das wandernde Gottesvolk: zum Basismotiv des Hebräerbriefes," *ZNW* 77 (1986): 160-79.

12:26-27

0443   A. Vogtle, "Die Gerichts- und Heilsansage von Hebr 12,26f.," in *Das Neue Testament und die Zukunft des Kosmos*. Düsseldorf: Patmos, 1970. Pp. 76-89.

13

0444   Robert Jewett, "Form and Function of the Homiletic Benediction," *ATR* 51 (1969): 18-34.

13:1-16
> **0445** Wolfgang Schenk, "Die Paränese Hebr 13:16 im Kontext des Hebräerbriefs: einer Fallstudie semiotisch-orientierter Textinterpretation und Sachkritik," *StTheol* 39 (1985): 73-106.

13:1-6
> **0446** Peter R. Jones, "A Superior Life: Hebrews 12:3-13:25," *RevExp* 82 (1985): 391-405.

13:4
> **0447** Lincoln D. Hurst, "Apollos, Hebrews, and Corinth: Bishop Montefiore's Theory Examined," *SJT* 38 (1985): 505-13.

13:5
> **0448** Peter Katz, "Hebrews 13:5: The Biblical Source of the Quotation," *Bib* 33 (1952): 523-25.

13:6
> **0449** Paul-Gerhard Müller, "Die Funktion der Psalmzitate im Hebräerbrief," Ernst Haag and F.-L. Hossfeld, eds., *Freude an der Weisung des Herrn: Beiträge zur Theologie der Psalmen* (festschrift for Heinrich Gross). Stuttgart: Verlag Katholisches Bibelwerk, 1986. Pp. 223-42.

13:7-17
> **0450** F. J. Schierse, "Altar und zukünftige Stadt," in *Verheissung und Heilsvollendung: Zur theologischen Grundfrage des Hebräerbriefes.* Münich: Zink, 1955. Pp. 185-95.

> **0451** Alois Stöger, "Leben aus dem Gottesdienst: Hebr 13:7-17," Heinz Schürmann, et al., eds., *Verbum caro factum est* (festschrift for Alois Stöger). Vienna, Austria: Niederösterreichisches Pressehaus, 1984. Pp. 35-38.

> **0452** Peter R. Jones, "A Superior Life: Hebrews 12:3-13:25," *RevExp* 82 (1985): 391-405.

13:7-16
> **0453** Gerald L. Borchert, "A Superior Book: Hebrews," *RevExp* 82 (1985): 319-22.

13:7

0454   H. Clavier, "*O logos tou theou* dans épître aux Hébreux," in A. J. B. Higgins, ed., *New Testament Essays* (festschrift for T. W. Manson). Manchester: University Prss, 1959. Pp. 81-93.

13:9-16

0455   Olaf Moe, "Das Abendmahl im Hebräerbrief: Zur Auslegung von Hebr 13:9-16," *StTheol* 4 (1950): 102-108.

13:9-14

0456   Helmut Koester, "Outside the Camp: Hebrews 13:9-14," *HTR* 55 (1962): 299-315.

0457   Peter Walker, "Jerusalem in Hebrews 13:9-14 and the Dating of the Epistle," *TynB* 45 (1994): 39-71.

13:10

0458   Antony Snell, "We Have an Altar," *RTR* 23 (1964): 16-23.

13:12-16

0459   Bengt Sundkler, "De sökte den tillkommande staden: Hebr 13:12-16," *Svensk Missionstidskrift* 49 (1961): 65-71.

13:15-16

0460   Vigen Guroian, "Seeing Worship as Ethics: An Orthodox Perspective," *JRE* 13 (1985): 332-59.

0461   A. Boyd Luter, "Worship as Service: The New Testament Usage of *latreuo*," *CTR* 2 (1988): 335-44.

13:17-19

0462   Lincoln D. Hurst, "Apollos, Hebrews, and Corinth: Bishop Montefiore's Theory Examined," *SJT* 38 (1985): 505-13.

13:17

0463   A. Burge Troxel, "Accountability without Bondage: Shepherd Leadership in the Biblical Church," *CEJ* 2 (1982): 39-46.

0464   Timothy M. Willis, " 'Obey Your Leaders': Hebrews 13 and Leadership in the Church," *RQ* 36 (1994): 316-26.

13:18-21

0465   Peter R. Jones, "A Superior Life: Hebrews 12:3-13:25," *RevExp* 82 (1985): 391-405.

13:20-21

0466   Charles E. B. Cranfield, "Hebrews 13:20-21," *SJT* 20 (1967): 437-41.

13:20

0467   Richard L. Mayhue, "Heb 13:20: Covenant of Grace or New Covenant? An Exegetical Note," *MSemJ* 7 (1996): 251-57.

13:22

0468   L. Paul Trudinger, *"Kai gar dia bracheon epesteila Hymin*: A Note on Hebrews 13:22," *JTS* NS 23 (1972): 128-30.

PART TWO

Citations by Subjects

Aaron

0469 William Horbury, "The Aaronic Priesthood in the Epistle to the Hebrews," *JSNT* 19 (1983): 43-71.

0470 Harold S. Songer, "A Superior Priesthood: Hebrews 4:14-7:27," *RevExp* 82 (1985): 345-59.

Abraham

0471 David G. Peterson, "Biblical Theology and the Argument of Hebrews," in Peterson John Pryor, eds., *In the Fullness of Time* (festschrift for Donald Robinson). Homebush West NSW: Lancer, 1992. Pp. 219-35.

allegory

0472 George MacRae, "A Kingdom that Cannot Be Shaken: The Heavenly Jerusalem in the Letter to the Hebrews," in Pierre Bonnard, et al., *Spirituality and Ecumenism*. Jerusalem: Ecumenical Institute for Theological Research, 1980. Pp. 27-40.

angels

0473 Edvin Larsson, "Sonen och änglarna i Hebr 1-2," in Ivar Asheim, et al., eds., *Israel, Kristus, kirken* (festschrift for Sverre Aalen). Oslo: Universitetsforlaget, 1979. Pp. 91-108.

anthropology

0474 Eugene F. Klug, "The Doctrine of Man: Christian Anthropology," *CTQ* 48 (1984): 141-52.

anti-semiticism

0475 William Klassen, "To the Hebrews or against the Hebrews: Anti-Judaism and the Epistle to the Hebrews," in Stephen Wilson, ed., *Anti-Judaism in Early Christianity*. Volume 2: *Separation and Polemic*. Studies in Christianity and Judaism #2. Waterloo, Ontario: Wilfried Laurier University Press, 1986. Pp. 1-16.

0476 J. C. McCullough, "Anti-Semitism in Hebrews?" *IBS* 20 (1998): 30-45.

apocalyptic

0477 Lincoln D. Hurst, "Eschatology and 'Platonism' in the Epistle to the Hebrews," *SBLSP* 23 (1984): 41-74.

Apollos of Alexandria

0478 A. M. Hunter, "Apollos the Alexandrian," in J. R. McKay J. F. Miller, eds., *Biblical Studies* (festschrift for William Barclay). Philadelphia: Westminster Press, 1976. Pp. 147-56.

apostacy

0479 Herbert H. Hohenstein, "Study of Hebrews 6:4-8: The Passage in the General Setting of the Whole Epistle," *CTM* 27 (1956): 433-44.

0480 Philip E. Hughes, "Hebrews 6:4-6 and the Peril of Apostasy," *WTJ* 35 (1973): 137-55.

0481 Alan Mugridge, "Warnings in the Epistle to the Hebrews: An Exegetical and Theological Study," *RTR* 46 (1987): 74-82.

0482 Wayne R. Kempson, "Hebrews 6:1-8," *RevExp* 91 (1994): 567-73.

atonement

0483 William M. F. Scott, "Priesthood in the New Testament," *SJT* 10 (1957): 399-415.

0484 James Swetnam, "On the Imagery and Significance of Hebrews 9:9-10," *CBQ* 28 (1966): 155-73.

0485 Ortensio Da Spinetoli, "Il senso della croce nella lettera agli Ebrei: portata storica e interpretazione teologica," in Christian Duquoc, et al., eds., *La sapienza della croce oggi, 1: la sapienza della croce nella rivelazione e nell'ecumenismo*. Turin: Elle Di Ci, 1976. Pp. 136-43.

0486 C. Samuel Storms, "Defining the Elect," *JETS* 27 (1984): 205-18.

0487 A. N. Chester, "Hebrews: The Final Sacrifice," in Stephen W. Sykes, ed., *Sacrifice and Redemption: Durham Essays in Theology*. Cambridge: University Press, 1991. Pp. 57-72.

0488 Barnabas Lindars, "Hebrews and the Second Temple," in William Horbury, ed., *Templum Amicitiae: Essays on the Second Temple* (festschrift for Ernst Bammel). Sheffield: JSOT Press, 1991. Pp. 410-33.

0489 Samuel Benetreau, "La mort de Jésus et le sacrifice dans l'épître aux Hébreux," *FV* 95 (1996): 33-45.

0490 T. G. Long, "Bold in the Presence of God. Atonement in Hebrews," *Int* 52 (1998): 53-69.

authority

0491 Timothy M. Willis, " 'Obey Your Leaders': Hebrews 13 and Leadership in the Church," *RQ* 36 (1994): 316-26.

baptism

0492 John Murray, "Christian Baptism," *WTJ* 13 (1951): 105-50.

0493 Gottfried Schille, "Katechese und Taufliturgie: Erwägungen zu Hbr 11," *ZNW* 51 (1960): 112-31.

0494 Vigen Guroian, "Seeing Worship as Ethics: An Orthodox Perspective," *JRE* 13 (1985): 332-59.

Cain and Abel

0495 Ceslaus Spicq, "L'Epître aux Hébreux et Philon: un cas d'insertion de la littérature sacrée dans la culture profane du Iuer Psiècle," in Wolfgang Haase, ed., *Principat 25, 4: Religion.* New York: Walter de Gruyter, 1987. Pp. 3602-18.

chiasmus

0496 David Alan Black, "A Note on the Structure of Hebrews 12:1-2," *Bib* 68 (1987): 543-51.

0497 V. Rhee, "Chiasm and the Concept of Faith in Hebrews 11," *BSac* 155 (1998): 327-45.

Christlogy

0498 Nils A. Dahl, "A New and Living Way: The Approach to God according to Hebrews 10:19-25," *Int* 5 (1951): 401-12.

0499 K. G. Kuhn, "Jesus in Gethsemane," *EvT* 12 (1952-1953): 260-85.

0500 August Strobel, "Die Psalmengrundlage der Gethsemane-Parallele, Hebr 5:7ff," *ZNW* 45 (1954): 252-66.

0501 J. C. Campbell, "In a Son: The Doctrine of Incarnation in the Epistle to the Hebrews," *Int* 10 (1956): 24-38.

0502   E. Käsemann, *"Das wandernde Gottesvolk": Eine Untersuchung zum Hebräerbrief.* FRLANT #37. Göttingen: Vandenhoeck & Ruprecht, 1961.

0503   U. Luck, "Himmlisches und irdisches Geschehen im Hebräerbrief: Ein Beitrag zum Problem des 'historischen Jesus' im Urchristentum," *NovT* 6 (1963): 192-215.

0504   H. Zimmerman, *Die Hohepriester -Christologic des Hebräerbriefes.* Paderborn: Schöningh, 1964.

0505   Erich Grässer, "Der historische Jesus im Hebräerbrief," *ZNW* 56 (1965): 63-91.

0506   Albert Vanhoye, "Christologia a qua initium sumit epistola ad Hebraeos," *VD* 43 (1965): 3-14, 49-61, 113-23.

0507   Theodor Lescow, "Jesus in Gethsemane bei Lukas und im Hebraerbrief," *ZNW* 58 (1967): 215-39.

0508   D. G. Miller, "Why God Became Man: From Text to Sermon on Hebrews 2:5-18," *Int* 23 (1969): 408-24.

0509   Frances M. Young, "Christological Ideas in the Greek Commentaries on the Epistle to the Hebrews," *JTS* NS 20 (1969): 150-63.

0510   James Swetnam, "Form and Content in Hebrews 1-6," *Bib* 53 (1972): 368-85.

0511   Erich Grässer, "Zur Christologie des Hebräerbriefes. Eine Auseinandersetiung mit Herbert Braun," in H. D. Betz and L Schottroff, eds., *Neues Testament und christhliche Existenz* (festschrift for Herbert Braun). Tübingen, Mohr, 1973. Pp. 195-206.

0512   A. Stadelmann, "Zur Christologie des Hebräerbriefes in der neueren Diskussion," in *Theologische Berichte II, Zur neueren christologischen Diskussion.* Zürich: Benziger, 1973. Pp. 135-321.

0513   Ronald Williamson, "Hebrews 4:15 and the Sinlessness of Jesus," *ET* 86 (1974): 4-8.

0514   Ronald H. Nash, "Notion of Mediator in Alexandrian Judaism and the Epistle to the Hebrews," *WTJ* 40 (1977): 89-115.

0515 Antonio Vicent Cernuda, "La introducción del Primogénito, según Hebr 1:6," *EB* NS 39 (1981): 107-53.

0516 Janusz Frankowski, "Early Christian Hymns Recorded in the New Testament: A Reconsideration of the Question in the Light of Hebrews 1:3," *BZ* NS 27 (1983): 183-94.

0517 Henk Jan de Jonge, "Traditie en exegese: de hogepriester-christologie en Melchizedek in Hebreeën," *NTT* 37 (1983): 1-19.

0518 Ronald Williamson, "The Incarnation of the Logos in Hebrews," *ET* 95 (1983): 4-8.

0519 Agustín del Agua Pérez, "Procedimientos derásicos del Sal 2:7b en el Nuevo Testamento: Tu eres mi hijo, yo te he engendrado hoy," *EB* NS 42 (1984): 391-414.

0520 George B. Caird, "Son by Appointment," in William C. Weinrich, ed., *The New Testament Age* (festschrift for Bo Reicke). 2 vols. Macon GA: Mercer Universitry Press, 1984. 1:73-81.

0521 Erich Grässer, "Mose und Jesus: zur Auslegung von Hebr 3:1-6," *ZNW* 75 (1984): 2-23.

0522 David G. Peterson, "Towards a New Testament Theology of Worship," *RTR* 43 (1984): 65-73.

0523 Palémon Glorieux, "La révélation du Pére," *MSR* 42 (1985): 21-41.

0524 John P. Meier, "Symmetry and Theology in the Old Testament Citations of Hebrews 1:5-14," *Bib* 66 (1985): 504-33.

0525 Thomas G. Smothers, "A Superior Model: Hebrews 1:1-4:13," *RevExp* 82 (1985): 333-43.

0526 Harold W. Attridge, "The Uses of Antithesis in Hebrews 8-10," in George W. E. Nickelsburg and George W. MacRae, eds., *Christians among Jews and Gentiles* (festschrift for Krister Stendahl). Philadelphia: Fortress Press, 1986. Pp. 1-9.

0527 Merland Ray Miller, "What is the Literary Form of Hebrews 11," *JETS* 29 (1986): 419-27.

0528   Stanley Frost, "Who Were the Heroes: An Exercise in Bi-testamentary Exegesis, with Christological Implications," in L. D. Hurst and Nicholas T. Wright, eds., *The Glory of Christ in the New Testament: Studies in Christology.* Oxford: Clarendon Press, 1987. Pp. 165-72.

0529   Lincoln D. Hurst, "The Christology of Hebrews 1 and 2," in L. D. Hurst and Nicholas T. Wright, eds., *The Glory of Christ in the New Testament: Studies in Christology.* Oxford: Clarendon Press, 1987. Pp. 151-64.

0530   Gabriel Josipovici, "The Epistle to the Hebrews and the Catholic Epistles," in Robert Alter and Frank Kermode, eds., *The Literary Guide to the Bible.* Cambridge MA: Harvard University Press, 1987. Pp. 503-22.

0531   David E. Aune, "Heracles and Christ: Heracles Imagery in the Christology of Early Christianity," in David L. Balch, et als., eds., *Greeks, Romans, and Christians* (festschrift for Abraham J. Malherbe. Minneapolis: Fortress Press, 1990. Pp. 3-19.

0532   Mario Caprioli, "Il sacerdozio di Cristo," in Antonio Piolanti, ed., *Atti del IX Congresso tomistico internazionale, 6: Storia del tomismo.* Vatican City: Libreria Editrice Vaticana, 1991. Pp. 96-105.

0533   A. N. Chester, "Hebrews: The Final Sacrifice," in Stephen W. Sykes, ed., *Sacrifice and Redemption: Durham Essays in Theology.* Cambridge: University Press, 1991. Pp. 57-72.

0534   Scott C. Layton, "Christ over His House (Hebrew 3:6) and Hebrew *'shr l-hbyt* [Gen 37-50, 1-2 Kgs]," *NTS* 37 (1991): 473-77.

0535   David J. MacLeod, "The Present Work of Christ in Hebrews," *BS* 148 (1991): 184-200.

0536   Enrique Nardoni, "Partakers in Christ (Hebrews 3:14)," *NTS* 37 (1991): 456-72.

0537   Claus P. März, "Vom Trost der Theologie: Zur Pragmatik der christologisch-soteriologischen Reflexion im Hebräerbrief," in Wilhem Ernst and Konrad Feiereis, eds., *Denkender Glaube im Geschichte und Gegenwart.* Erfurter theologische Studien #63. Leipzig: Benno-Verlag, 1992. Pp. 260-76.

0538   Mark Saucy, "Exaltation Christology in Hebrews: What Kind of Reign?" *TriJ* 14 (1993): 41-62.

0539   Otfried Hofius, "Biblische Theologie im Lichte des Hebräerbriefes," in Sigfred Pedersen, ed., *New Directions in Biblical Theology*. Leiden: Brill, 1994. Pp. 108-25.

0540   Gerd Schunack, "Jesu 'Opfertod' im Hebräerbrief," in Ulrich Schoenborn and Stephan Pfürtner, eds., *Der bezwingende Vorsprung des Guten: exegetische und theologische Werkstattberichte* (festschrift for Wolfgang Harnisch). Munster: Lit, 1994. Pp. 209-31.

0541   Roger T. Beckwith, "The Death of Christ as a Sacrifice in the Teaching of Paul and Hebrews," in Roger T. Beckwith and Martin J. Selman, eds., *Sacrifice in the Bible*. Grand Rapids: Baker Book House, 1995. Pp. 130-35.

0542   Pamela Bright, "The Epistle to the Hebrews in Origen's Christology," in Gilles Dorival and Alain Le Boulluec, eds., *Origeniana sexta: Origène et la Bible*. Louvain: Peeters, 1995. Pp. 559-65.

0543   Christopher Cocksworth, "The Cross, Our Worship and Our Living," in John Goldingay, ed., *Atonement Today: A Symposium at St. John's College, Nottingham*. London: SPCK, 1995. Pp. 111-27.

0544   Samuel Benetreau, "La mort de Jésus et le sacrifice dans l'épître aux Hébreux," *FV* 95 (1996): 33-45.

0545   Albert Vanhoye, "La '*teleiôsis*' du Christ," *NTS* 42 (1996): 321-38.

0546   Bernhard Heininger, "Sündenreinigung (Hebr 1,3): Christologie Anmerkungen zum Exordium des Hebräerbriefs," *BZ* NS 41 (1997): 54-68.

0547   Kenneth Schenck, "Keeping His Appointment: Creation and Enthronement in Hebrews," *JSNT* 66 (1997): 91-117.

0548   Albert Vanhoye, "La novitá del sacerdozio di Cristo," *CivCatt* 149 (1998): 16-27.

cosmology
> **0549** Paul Ellingworth, "Jesus and the Universe in Hebrews," *EQ* 58 (1986): 337-350.

covenant/covenants
> **0550** K. M. Campbell, "Covenant or Testament? Hebrews 9:16,17 Reconsidered," *EQ* 44 (1972): 107-111.

> **0551** Andrew T. Lincoln, "Sabbath, Rest, and Eschatology in the New Testament," in Don A. Carson, ed., *From Sabbath to Lord's Day: A Biblical, Historical and Theological Investigation.* Grand Rapids MI: Zondervan Publishing House, 1982. Pp. 198-220.

> **0552** Jean P. Michaud, "Le passage de l'ancien au nouveau, selon l'épître aux Hébreux," *SE* 35 (1983): 33-52.

> **0553** Roger L. Omanson, "A Superior Covenant: Hebrews 8:1-10:18," *RevExp* 82 (1985): 361-73.

> **0554** William Klassen, "To the Hebrews or against the Hebrews: Anti-Judaism and the Epistle to the Hebrews," in Stephen Wilson, ed., *Anti-Judaism in Early Christianity.* Volume 2: *Separation and Polemic.* Studies in Christianity and Judaism #2. Waterloo, Ontario: Wilfried Laurier University Press, 1986. Pp. 1-16.

> **0555** Stanley Frost, "Who Were the Heroes: An Exercise in Bi-testamentary Exegesis, with Christological Implications," in L. D. Hurst and Nicholas T. Wright, eds., *The Glory of Christ in the New Testament: Studies in Christology.* Oxford: Clarendon Press, 1987. Pp. 165-72.

> **0556** Gabriel Josipovici, "The Epistle to the Hebrews and the Catholic Epistles," in Robert Alter and Frank Kermode, eds., *The Literary Guide to the Bible.* Cambridge MA: Harvard University Press, 1987. Pp. 503-22.

> **0557** Susanne Lehne, *The New Covenant in Hebrews.* Sheffield: JSOT Press, 1990.

> **0558** John Dunnill, *Covenant and Sacrifice in the Letter to the Hebrews.* Cambridge: University Press, 1992.

> **0559** Richard L. Mayhue, "Heb 13:20: Covenant of Grace or New Covenant? An Exegetical Note," *MSemJ* 7 (1996): 251-57.

creation
>
> **0560** Klaus Haacker, "Creatio ex auditu: zum Verstandnis von Hbr 11:3," *ZNW* 60 (1969): 279-81.

crucifixion
>
> **0561** James K. Elliott, "When Jesus Was Apart from God: An Examination of Hebrews 2:9," *ET* 83 (1972): 339-41.
>
> **0562** Ortensio Da Spinetoli, "Il senso della croce nella lettera agli Ebrei: portata storica e interpretazione teologica," in Christian Duquoc, et al., eds., *La sapienza della croce oggi, 1: la sapienza della croce nella rivelazione e nell'ecumenismo*. Turin: Elle Di Ci, 1976. Pp. 136-43.
>
> **0563** Ferdinand Hahn, "Das Verständnis des Opfers im Neuen Testament," in Karl Lehmann and Edmund Schlink, *Das Opfer Jesu Christi und seine Gegenwart in der Kirche: Klärungen zum Opfercharakter des Herrenmahles*. Dialog Der kirchen #3. Freiburg: Herder, 1983. Pp. 51-91.
>
> **0564** Albert Vanhoye, "Esprit éternel et feu du sacrifice en He 9:14," *Bib* 64 (1983): 263-274.
>
> **0565** Harold W. Attridge, "The Uses of Antithesis in Hebrews 8-10," in George W. E. Nickelsburg and George W. MacRae, eds., *Christians among Jews and Gentiles* (festschrift for Krister Stendahl). Philadelphia: Fortress Press, 1986. Pp. 1-9.
>
> **0566** Armando J. Levoratti, "Tú no has querido sacrificio ni oblación: Salmo 40:7; Hebreos 10:5; pt 2," *RevB* 48 (1986): 193-237.
>
> **0567** Franz Laub, "Ein für allemal hineingegangen in das Allerheiligste (Hebr 9:12)--zum Verständnis des Kreuzestodes im Hebräerbrief," *BZ* NS 35 (1991): 65-85.
>
> **0568** Gerd Schunack, "Jesu 'Opfertod' im Hebräerbrief," in Ulrich Schoenborn and Stephan Pfürtner, eds., *Der bezwingende Vorsprung des Guten: exegetische und theologische Werkstattberichte* (festschrift for Wolfgang Harnisch). Munster: Lit, 1994. Pp. 209-31.
>
> **0569** Roger T. Beckwith, "The Death of Christ as a Sacrifice in the Teaching of Paul and Hebrews," in Roger T. Beckwith and Martin J.

Selman, eds., *Sacrifice in the Bible*. Grand Rapids: Baker Book House, 1995. Pp. 130-35.

0570   Samuel Benetreau, "La mort de Jésus et le sacrifice dans l'épître aux Hébreux," *FV* 95 (1996): 33-45.

cult

0571   M. Dibelius, "Der himmlische Kultus nach dem Hebräerbrief," *TBl* 21 (1942): 1-20.

0572   F. J. Schierse, "Das himmlische Heiligtum," *Verheissung und Heilsvollendung: Zur theologischen Grundfrage des Hebräerbriefes*. Münich: Zink, 1955. Pp. 13-64.

0573   A. Cody, *Heavenly Sanctuary and Liturgy in the Epistle to the Hebrews. The Achievement of Salvation in the Epistle's Perspective*. St. Meinrad: Grail Publications, 1960.

0574   W. Stott, "The Conception of 'Offering' in the Epistle to the Hebrews," *NTS* 9 (1962-1963): 62-67.

0575   Friedrick Schröger, "Der Gottesdienst der Hebräerbriefgemeinde," *MüTZ* 19 (1968): 161-81.

0576   W. E. Brooks, "The Perpetuity of Christ's Sacrifice in the Epistle to the Hebrews," *JBL* 89 (1970): 205-14.

0577   J. Delorme, "Sacrifice, sacercloce, consecration: Typologic el analyse semantique du discours," *RechSR* 63 (1975): 343-68.

0578   David G. Peterson, "Towards a New Testament Theology of Worship," *RTR* 43 (1984): 65-73.

0579   David G. Peterson, "Further Reflections on Worship in the New Testament," *RTR* 44 (1985): 34-41.

0580   Darrell Pursiful, *The Cultic Motif in the Spirituality of the Book of Hebrews*. Lewiston NY: Mellen Biblical Press, 1993.

0581   A. Craig Troxel, " 'Cleansed Once for All': John Owen on the Glory of Gospel Worship in 'Hebrews'," *CTJ* 32 (1997): 468-79.

death

0582 Edward Fudge, "The Final End of the Wicked," *JETS* 27 (1984): 325-34.

determinism

0583 John D. Madden, "The Authenticity of Early Definitions of Will," in Felix Heinzer and Chris Schönborn, eds., *Maximus Confessor.* Fribourg: Editions Universitaires, 1982. Pp. 61-79.

deutero-Pauline hypothesis

0584 Knut Backhaus, "Der Hebräerbrief und die Paulus-Schule," *BZ* NS 37 (1993): 183-208.

discipleship

0585 William L. Lane, "Standing before the Moral Claim of God: Discipleship in Hebrews," in Richard N. Longenecker, ed., *Patterns of Discipleship in the New Testament.* Grand Rapids: Eerdmans, 1996. Pp. 203-24.

discourse analysis

0586 David Alan Black, "Hebrews 1:1-4: A Study in Discourse Analysis," *WTJ* 49 (1987): 175-94.

0587 Linda Lloyd-Neeley, "A Discourse Analysis of Hebrews," *OPTAT* (1987): 1-146.

dualism

0588 Jeffrey R. Sharp, "Philonism and the Eschatology of Hebrews: Another Look," *EAJT* 2 (1984): 289-98.

Ebionism

0589 Robert W. Thurston, "Philo and the Epistle to the Hebrews," *EQ* 58 (1986): 133-43.

ecclesiology

0590 T. da Castel, *La chiesa nella letter agli Ebrei.* Rome: Marielti, 1945.

0591 John Murray, "Christian Baptism," *WTJ* 13 (1951): 105-50.

0592 J. Morin, "L'Eglise clans l'épître aux Hébreux," in *L'Église dans la Bible.* Bruges: Deslée de Brouwer, 1962. Pp. 117-27.

0593 H. Schlier, "Die Kirche nach dem Hebräerbrief," in J. Feiner and M. Löhrer, eds., *Mysterium Salutis.* Volume 4. Einsiedeln: Benziger, 1972. Pp. 187-94.

0594 E. A. C. Pretorius, "Christusbeeld en Kerkmodel in die Hebreërbrief," *ThEv* 15 (1982): 3-6.

0595 A. Burge Troxel, "Accountability without Bondage: Shepherd Leadership in the Biblical Church," *CEJ* 2 (1982): 39-46.

0596 Erich Grässer, "Mose und Jesus: zur Auslegung von Hebr 3:1-6," *ZNW* 75 (1984): 2-23.

0597 Rolf Gögler, "Inkarnationsglaube und Bibeltheologie bei Origenes," *TQ* 165 (1985): 82-94.

0598 François Marty, "Le péché sans rémission dans l'epître aux Hébreux," in Michel Perrin, ed., *Le pardon: actes du colloque organisé par le Centre histoire des idées Université de Picardie.* Le Point théologique #45. Paris: Beauchesne, 1987. Pp. 29-47.

elders

0599 A. Burge Troxel, "Accountability without Bondage: Shepherd Leadership in the Biblical Church," *CEJ* 2 (1982): 39-46.

0600 Timothy M. Willis, " 'Obey Your Leaders': Hebrews 13 and Leadership in the Church," *RQ* 36 (1994): 316-26.

eschatology

0601 C. K. Barrett, "The Eschatology of the Epistle to the Hebrews," in W. D. Davies and D. Daube, eds., *The Background of the New Testament and Its Eschatology* (festschrift for C. H. Dodd). Cambridge: University Press, 1964. Pp. 363-93.

0602 Tomasz Jelonek, "Palpabile et 'Mons Sion': de vero sensu antithesis in Hbr 12,18-24," in Adam Kubis, et al., , *Analecta Cracoviensia, 1977.* Krakow: Polskie Towarzystwo Teologiczne, 1977. Pp. 139-54.

0603 Andrew T. Lincoln, "Sabbath, Rest, and Eschatology in the New Testament," in Don A. Carson, ed., *From Sabbath to Lord's Day: A Biblical, Historical and Theological Investigation.* Grand Rapids MI: Zondervan Publishing House, 1982. Pp. 198-220.

0604   Edward Fudge, "The Final End of the Wicked," *JETS* 27 (1984): 325-34.

0605   Erich Grässer, "Mose und Jesus: zur Auslegung von Hebr 3:1-6," *ZNW* 75 (1984): 2-23.

0606   Lincoln D. Hurst, "Eschatology and 'Platonism' in the Epistle to the Hebrews," *SBLSP* 23 (1984): 41-74.

0607   Daniel R. Mitchell, "Man on the Eve of Destruction," *FundJ* 3 (1984): 23-27.

0608   Jeffrey R. Sharp, "Philonism and the Eschatology of Hebrews: Another Look," *EAJT* 2 (1984): 289-98.

0609   Luis F. Ladaria, "Presente y futuro en la escatología cristiana," *EE* 60 (1985): 351-59.

0610   H. Anderson, "The Jewish Antecedents of the Christology in Hebrews," in James H. Charlesworth, ed., *The Messiah: Developments in Earliest Judaism and Christianity*. Minneapolis: Fortress Press, 1992. Pp. 512-35.

ethics

0611   John F. Jansen, "Commitment: A Perspective from the New Testament," *ASemB* 87 (1972): 20-31.

0612   Jeffery Gibbs, "The Grace of God as the Foundation for Ethics," *CTQ* 48 (1984): 185-201.

0613   Vigen Guroian, "Seeing Worship as Ethics: An Orthodox Perspective," *JRE* 13 (1985): 332-59.

0614   Wolfgang Schenk, "Die Paränese Hebr 13:16 im Kontext des Hebräerbriefs: einer Fallstudie semiotisch-orientierter Textinterpretation und Sachkritik," *StTheol* 39 (1985): 73-106.

0615   Thomas E. Schmidt, "Moral Lethargy and the Epistle to the Hebrews," *WTJ* 54 (1992): 167-73.

exodus

0616   Albert Vanhoye, "Longue marche ou accès tout proche? Le contexte biblique de Hébreux 3:7-4:11," *Bib* 49 (1968): 9-26.

faith

0617 Otto Küster, "Konkreter Glaube," *ZTK* 48 (1951): 101-14.

0618 Erich Grässer, *Der Glaube im Hebräerbrief.* Marburg: Elwert Verlag, 1965.

0619 G. Dautzenberg, "Der Glaube in Hebräerbrief," *BZ* 17 (1973): 161-77.

0620 C. Perrot, "L'Épître aux Hébreux," in *Le ministère et les ministères selon le Nouveau Testament.* Paris: Seuil, 1974. 2:8-137.

0621 George Duncan, "Obedience and Faith," in David Porter, ed., *The People and the King.* Bromley, England: Send the Light Trust, 1980. Pp. 122-127

0622 Klaus Haacker, "Der Glaube im Hebräerbrief und die hermeneutische Bedeutung des Holocaust," *TZ* 39 (1983): 152-65.

0623 R. Alan Culpepper, "A Superior Faith: Hebrews 10:19-12:2," *RevExp* 82 (1985): 375-90.

0624 Otto Betz, "Firmness in faith: Hebrews 11:1 and Isaiah 28:16," in Barry P. Thompson, ed., *Scripture: Meaning and Method:.* (festschrift for A. T. Hanson). Hull UK: Hull University Press, 1987. Pp. 92-113.

0625 Stanley Frost, "Who Were the Heroes: An Exercise in Bi-testamentary Exegesis, with Christological Implications," in L. D. Hurst and Nicholas T. Wright, eds., *The Glory of Christ in the New Testament: Studies in Christology.* Oxford: Clarendon Press, 1987. Pp. 165-72.

0626 Vincent Harding, "In the Company of the Faithful: Journeying toward the Promised Land," in Jim Wallis, ed,, *The Rise of Christian Conscience: The Emergence of a Dramatic Renewal Movement in the Church Today.* San Francisco: Harper and Row, 1987. Pp. 273-84.

0627 Gabriel Josipovici, "The Epistle to the Hebrews and the Catholic Epistles," in Robert Alter and Frank Kermode, eds., *The Literary Guide to the Bible.* Cambridge MA: Harvard University Press, 1987. Pp. 503-22.

0628 Richard A. Spencer, "Hebrews 11:1-3, 8-16," *Int* 49 (1995): 288-92.

0629 Kimberly F. Baker, "Hebrews 11--The Promise of Faith," *RevExp* 94 (1997): 439-45.

free will
0630 John D. Madden, "The Authenticity of Early Definitions of Will," in Felix Heinzer and Chris Schönborn, eds., *Maximus Confessor.* Fribourg: Editions Universitaires, 1982. Pp. 61-79.

grace
0631 Jeffery Gibbs, "The Grace of God as the Foundation for Ethics," *CTQ* 48 (1984): 185-201.

harmartology
0632 Jeffery Gibbs, "The Grace of God as the Foundation for Ethics," *CTQ* 48 (1984): 185-201.

0633 François Marty, "Le péché sans rémission dans l'epître aux Hébreux," in Michel Perrin, ed., *Le pardon: actes du colloque organisé par le Centre histoire des idées Université de Picardie.* Le Point théologique #45. Paris: Beauchesne, 1987. Pp. 29-47.

heaven
0634 Olaf Moe, "Das irdische und das himmlische Heiligtum: Zur Auslegung von Hebr 9:4f," *TZ* 9 (1953): 23-29.

0635 David J. MacLeod, "The Cleansing of the True Tabernacle," *BSac* 152 (1995): 60-71.

Hellenistic influence
0636 Lincoln D. Hurst, "How 'Platonic' Are Hebrews 8:5 and Hebrews 9:23f?" *JTS* NS 34 (1983): 156-68.

0637 F. F. Bruce, "To the Hebrews: A Document of Roman Christianity," in Wolfgang Haase, ed., *Principat 25, 4: Religion.* New York: Walter de Gruyter, 1987. Pp. 3496-3521.

0638 Helmut Feld, "Der Hebräerbrief: literarische Form, religionsgeschichtlicher Hintergrund, theologische Fragen," in Wolfgang Haase, ed., *Principat 25, 4: Religion.* New York: Walter de Gruyter, 1987. Pp. 3522-3601

0639 Ceslaus Spicq, "L'Epître aux Hébreux et Philon: un cas d'insertion de la littérature sacrée dans la culture profane du Iuer Psiècle," in Wolfgang Haase, ed., *Principat 25, 4: Religion.* New York: Walter de Gruyter, 1987. Pp. 3602-18.

0640 Jerome H. Neyrey, "Without Beginning of Days or End of Life (Hebrews 7:3): Topos for a True Deity," *CBQ* 53 (1991): 439-55.

0641 H. Anderson, "The Jewish Antecedents of the Christology in Hebrews," in James H. Charlesworth, ed., *The Messiah: Developments in Earliest Judaism and Christianity.* Minneapolis: Fortress Press, 1992. Pp. 512-35.

Holiness
0642 Peter R. Jones, "A Superior Life: Hebrews 12:3-13:25," *RevExp* 82 (1985): 391-405.

Holy Spirit
0643 John Murray, "Christian Baptism," *WTJ* 13 (1951): 105-50.

0644 Albert Vanhoye, "Esprit éternel et feu du sacrifice en He 9:14," *Bib* 64 (1983): 263-274.

hope
0645 Daniel R. Mitchell, "Man on the Eve of Destruction," *FundJ* 3 (1984): 23-27.

hymns
0646 Paul Ellingworth, "Like the Son of God: Form and Content in Hebrews 7:1-10," *Bib* 64 (1983): 255-262.

0647 Janusz Frankowski, "Early Christian Hymns Recorded in the New Testament: A Reconsideration of the Question in the Light of Hebrews 1:3," *BZ* NS 27 (1983): 183-94.

0648 John P. Meier, "Symmetry and Theology in the Old Testament Citations of Hebrews 1:5-14," *Bib* 66 (1985): 504-33.

0649 Alan D. Bulley, "Death and Rhetoric in the Hebrews 'Hymn to Faith'," *SR* 25 (1996): 409-23.

inspiration
> **0650** Rolf Gögler, "Inkarnationsglaube und Bibeltheologie bei Origenes," *TQ* 165 (1985): 82-94.

introduction
> **0651** J. F. McFadyen, "The Message of the Epistles - Hebrews," *ET* 45 (1933-1934): 312-19.

> **0652** G. A. Barton, "The Date of the Epistle to the Hebrews," *JBL* 57 (1938): 195-207.

> **0653** I. Logan, "The Epistle to the Hebrews: An Expository Study," *ET* 50 (1938-1939): 39-42.

> **0654** L. O. Bristol, "Primitive Christian Preaching and the Epistle to the Hebrews," *JBL* 68 (1949): 89-97.

> **0655** T. W. Manson, "The Problem of the Epistle to the Hebrews," *BJRL* 32 (1949-1950): 1-17.

> **0656** W. F. Howard, "The Epistle to the Hebrews," *Int* 5 (1951): 80-91.

> **0657** Floyd V. Filson, "Epistle to the Hebrews," *JBR* 22 (1954): 20-26.

> **0658** E. J. Goodspeed, "The Problem of Hebrews," *JBR* 22 (1954): 122.

> **0659** R. McL. Wilson, "Coptisms in the Epistle to the Hebrews?" *NovT* 1 (1956): 322-24.

> **0660** C. P. M. Jones, "The Epistle to the Hebrews and the Lucan Writings," in D. E. Nineham, ed., *Studies in the Gospels* (festschrift for R. H. Lightfoot). Oxford: Blackwell, 1957. Pp. 113-43.

> **0661** Gottfried Schille, "Die Basis des Hebräerbriefes," *ZNW* 48 (1957): 270-90.

> **0662** Albert Vanhoye, *Traduction structurée de l'Épître aux Hébreux*. Rome: Institut Biblique Pontifical, 1963.

> **0663** W. Nauck, "Zum Aufbau des Hebräerbriefes," in Walther Eltester, ed., *Judentum, Urchristentuni, Kirche* (festschrift for Joachim Jeremias). BNZW #26. Berlin: Töpelmann, 1964. Pp. 199-206.

0664 R. A. Stewart, "Creation and Matter in the Epistie to the Hebrews," *NTS* 12 (1965-1966): 284-93.

0665 Charles P. Anderson, "The Epistle to the Hebrews and the Pauline Letter Collection," *HTR* 59 (1966): 429-38.

0666 S. Zedda, "La lettere agli Ebrei," in *Il messaggio della salvezza*. 5 volumes. Elle di ci: Torino-Leumann, 1966-1970. 5:812-37.

0667 James Swetnam, "On the Literary Genre of the 'Epistle' to the Hebrews," *NovT* 11 (1969): 261-69.

0668 Ronald Williamson, "Hebrews and Doctrine," *ET* 81 (1969-1970): 371-76.

0669 Royal Sage, "Paul the Author of Hebrews?" in Vern Carner and Gary Stanhiser, eds., *The Stature of Christ* (festschrift for Edward Heppenstall). Loma Linda CA: Carner and Stanhiser, 1970. Pp. 122-26.

0670 H. Braun, "Die Gewinnung der Gewissheit in dem Hebräerbriel," *TLZ* 96 (1971): 321-30.

0671 W. A. van Roo, "The Epistle to the Hebrews," in *The Mystery*. Rome: Georgian University Press, 1971. Pp. 135-43.

0672 G. Mora, *La carta a los Hebreos como escrito pastoral*. Herder: Barcelona, 1974.

0673 G. W. Buchanan, "The Present State of Scholarship on Hebrews," in Jacob Neunser, ed., *Christianity, Judaism and Other Greco-Roman Cults* (festschrift for Morton Smith). Volume 1: *New Testament*. Leiden: Brill, 1975. 1:299-330.

0674 A. M. Hunter, "Apollos the Alexandrian," in J. R. McKay J. F. Miller, eds., *Biblical Studies* (festschrift for William Barclay). Philadelphia: Westminster Press, 1976. Pp. 147-56.

0675 Ronald H. Nash, "Notion of Mediator in Alexandrian Judaism and the Epistle to the Hebrews," *WTJ* 40 (1977): 89-115.

0676 H. Zimmermann, *Das Bekenntnis der Hoffnung. Tradition und Redaktion im Hebräerbrief*. BBB #47. Köln: Hanstein, 1977.

0677   Albert Vanhoye, "Literarische Struktur und theologische Botschaft des Hebräerbriefs," *SNTU-A* 4 (1979): 119-47.

0678   Friedrich Schröger, "Der Hebraeerbrief: Paulinisch?" in Paul G. Mueller and Werner Stenger, eds., *Kontinuitaet und Einheit* (festschrift for Franz Mussner). Freiburg: Herder, 1981. Pp. 211-22.

0679   Herbert W. Chilstrom, *Hebrews: A New and Better Way*. Philadelphia: Fortress Press, 1984.

0680   Gerald L. Borchert, "A Superior Book: Hebrews," *RevExp* 82 (1985): 319-22.

0681   Lincoln D. Hurst, "Apollos, Hebrews, and Corinth: Bishop Montefiore's Theory Examined," *SJT* 38 (1985): 505-13.

0682   Robert W. Thurston, "Philo and the Epistle to the Hebrews," *EQ* 58 (1986): 133-43.

0683   Helmut Feld, "Der Hebräerbrief: literarische Form, religionsgeschichtlicher Hintergrund, theologische Fragen," in Wolfgang Haase, ed., *Principat 25, 4: Religion*. New York: Walter de Gruyter, 1987. Pp. 3522-3601

0684   B. P. Hunt, "The 'Epistle to the Hebrews': An Anti-judaic Treatise?" *StudE* 2 (1987): 408-10.

0685   M. Rissi, *Die Theologie des Hebräerbriefs: ihre Verankerung in der Situation des Verfassers und seiner Leser*. WUNT #41. Tübingen: Mohr, 1987.

0686   J. David Thompson, *A Critical Concordance to the Letter to the Hebrews*. The Computer Bible #29. Wooster OH: Biblical Research Associates, 1988.

0687   Charles P. Anderson, "Who Are the Heirs of the New Age in the Epistle to the Hebrews?" in Joel Marcus and Marion Soards, eds., *Apocalyptic and the New Testament* (festschrift for J. Louis Martyn). Sheffield: JSOT Press, 1989. Pp. 255-77.

0688   Lincoln D. Hurst, *The Epistle to the Hebrews: Its Background of Thought*. Cambridge: University Press, 1990.

0689   Robert B. Shaw, "The Epistle of Paul the Apostle to the Hebrews,"
in Alfred Corn, ed., *Incarnation: Contemporary Writers on the New
Testament*. New York: Viking, 1990. Pp. 265-80.

0690   Erich Grässer, "Neue Kommentare zum Hebräerbrief," *TR* 56 (1991):
113-39.

0691   Nello Casalini, *Agli Ebrei: discorso di esortazione*. Jerusalem:
Franciscan Printing Press, 1992.

0692   Knut Backhaus, "Der Hebräerbrief und die Paulus-Schule," *BZ* NS 37
(1993): 183-208.

0693   Robert M. Grant, "Ancient and Modern Questions about
Authenticity," in Bradley H. McLean, ed., *Origins and Method:
Towards a New Understanding of Judaism and Christianity*
(festschrift for John C. Hurd). Sheffield UK: JSOT Press, 1993. Pp.
295-301.

0694   Cyril S. Rodd, "Hebrews to Revelation: Recent Commentaries, part
4," *ET* 104 (1993): 236-38.

0695   Werner Vogler, "Johannes und der Hebräerbrief," *TheoV* 18 (1993):
83-97.

0696   David Alan Black, "Literary Artistry in the Epistle to the Hebrews,"
FilN 7 (1994): 43-51.

0697   David A. DeSilva, "Despising Shame: A Cultural-Anthropological
Investigation of the Epistle to the Hebrews," *JBL* 113 (1994): 439-61.

0698   Steve Stanley, "The Structure of Hebrews from Three Perspectives,"
TynB 45 (1994): 245-71.

0699   Peter Walker, "Jerusalem in Hebrews 13:9-14 and the Dating of the
Epistle," *TynB* 45 (1994): 39-71.

0700   Paul S. Minear, *The Golgotha Earthquake: Three Witnesses*.
Cleveland OH: Pilgrim Press, 1995.

0701   David L. Allen, "The Lukan Authorship of Hebrews," *JOTT* 8 (1996):
1-22.

0702 Marie E. Isaacs, "Hebrews," in John M. G. Barclay and John P. M. Sweet, eds., *Early Christian Thought in Its Jewish Context* (festschrift for Morna D. Hooker). New York: Cambridge University Press, 1996. Pp. 145-59.

0703 Andrew H. Trotter, *Interpreting the Epistle to the Hebrews.* Guides to New Testament Exegesis #6. Grand Rapids: Baker Books, 1997.

Jerusalem (symbol)

0704 Tomasz Jelonek, "Palpabile et 'Mons Sion': de vero sensu antithesis in Hbr 12,18-24," in Adam Kubis, et al., , *Analecta Cracoviensia, 1977.* Krakow: Polskie Towarzystwo Teologiczne, 1977. Pp. 139-54.

0705 George MacRae, "A Kingdom that Cannot Be Shaken: The Heavenly Jerusalem in the Letter to the Hebrews," in Pierre Bonnard, et al., *Spirituality and Ecumenism.* Jerusalem: Ecumenical Institute for Theological Research, 1980. Pp. 27-40.

0706 Lincoln D. Hurst, "Eschatology and 'Platonism' in the Epistle to the Hebrews," *SBLSP* 23 (1984): 41-74.

0707 Harold S. Camacho, "The Altar of Incense in Hebrews 9:3-4," *AUSS* 24 (1986): 5-12.

John, Gospel of

0708 Colin J. A. Hickling, "John and Hebrews: The Background of Hebrews 2:10-18," *NTS* 29 (1983): 112-16.

kerygma

0709 F. F. Bruce, "The Kerygma of Hebrews," *Int* 23 (1969): 3-19.

law

0710 William Klassen, "The King as 'Living Law' with Particular Reference to Musonius Rufus," *SR* 14 (1985): 63-71.

logos

0711 Ronald Williamson, "The Incarnation of the Logos in Hebrews," *ET* 95 (1983): 4-8.

Lord's Supper

0712 Olaf Moe, "Das Abendmahl im Hebräerbrief: Zur Auslegung von Hebr 13:9-16," *StTheol* 4 (1950): 102-108.

0713 James Swetnam, "Greater and More Perfect Tent: A Contribution to the Discussion of Hebrews 9:11," *Bib* 47 (1966): 91-106.

0714 P. Andriessen, "L'Eucharistie dans l'Épître aux Hébreux," *NRT* 94 (1972): 269-77.

0715 Ronald Williamson, "The Eucharist and the Epistle to the Hebrews," *NTS* 21 (1974-1975): 300-12.

0716 Vigen Guroian, "Seeing Worship as Ethics: An Orthodox Perspective," *JRE* 13 (1985): 332-59.

0717 David G. Peterson, "Further Reflections on Worship in the New Testament," *RTR* 44 (1985): 34-41.

0718 Albert Vanhoye, "Anamnèse historique et créativité théologique dans l'épître aux Hébreux," in Daniel Marguerat and Jean Zumstein, eds., *La mémoire et le temps* (festschrift for Pierre Bonnard). Le monde de la Bible #23. Geneva: Labor et Fides, 1991. Pp. 219-31.

0719 Otto Knoch, "Hält der Verfasser des Hebräerbriefs die Feier eucharistischer Gottesdienste für theologisch unangemessen?" *LitJ* 42 (1992): 166-87.

melchizedek
0720 Joseph A. Fitzmyer, "Now this Melchizedek," *CBQ* 25 (1963): 305-21.

0721 R. A. Stewart, "The Sinless High-Priest," *NTS* 14 (1967-1968): 126-35.

0722 Albert Vanhoye, "La figure de Melchisedek," in *Prêtres anciens, prêtre nouveau selon le Nouveau Testament*. Paris: Seuil, 1980. Pp. 171-93.

0723 Paul Ellingworth, "Like the Son of God: Form and Content in Hebrews 7:1-10," *Bib* 64 (1983): 255-262.

0724 Henk Jan de Jonge, "Traditie en exegese: de hogepriester-christologie en Melchizedek in Hebreeën," *NTT* 37 (1983): 1-19.

0725 Harold S. Songer, "A Superior Priesthood: Hebrews 4:14-7:27," *RevExp* 82 (1985): 345-59.

0726   Mark Kiley, "Melchisedek's Promotion to Archiereus and the Translation of *ta stoicheia tes arches*," *SBLSP* 25 (1986): 236-45.

0727   Gabriel Josipovici, "The Epistle to the Hebrews and the Catholic Epistles," in Robert Alter and Frank Kermode, eds., *The Literary Guide to the Bible*. Cambridge MA: Harvard University Press, 1987. Pp. 503-22.

0728   M. J. Paul, "The Order of Melchizedek (Ps 110:4 and Heb 7:3)," *WTJ* 49 (1987): 195-211.

0729   George H. Tavard, "The Meaning of Melchizedek for Contemporary Ministry," in Earl E. Shelp and Ronald H. Sunderland, eds., *The Pastor as Priest*. New York: Pilgrim Press, 1987. Pp. 64-85.

0730   Jerome H. Neyrey, "Without Beginning of Days or End of Life (Hebrews 7:3): Topos for a True Deity," *CBQ* 53 (1991): 439-55.

0731   Theo C. de Kruijf, "The Priest-King Melchizedek: The Reception of Gen 14,18-20 in Hebrews Mediated by Psalm 110," *Bij* 54 (1993): 393-406.

messianism
0732   Herbert W. Bateman, "Two First-Century Messianic Uses of the OT: Hebrews 1:5-13 and 4QFlor 1.1-19," *JETS* 38 (1995): 11-27.

Midrash
0733   Paul-Gerhard Müller, "Die Funktion der Psalmzitate im Hebräerbrief," in Ernst Haag and F.-L. Hossfeld, eds., *Freude an der Weisung des Herrn: Beiträge zur Theologie der Psalmen* (festschrift for Heinrich Gross). Stuttgart: Verlag Katholisches Bibelwerk, 1986. Pp. 223-42.

0734   David Flusser, "Today If You Will Listen to This Voice: Creative Exegesis in Hebrews 3-4," in Benjamin Uffenheimer, et al., eds., - *Creative Biblical Exegesis: Christian and Jewish Hermeneutics through the Centuries*. Sheffield: JSOT Press, 1988. Pp. 55-62.

missions
0735   Robert Smith, "The Rise of the Christian World Mission," *IRM* 43 (1954): 330-35.

0736   Mark R. Shaw, "Is There Salvation outside the Christian Faith," *EAJT* 2 (1983): 42-62.

Moses

0737 E. A. C. Pretorius, "Christusbeeld en Kerkmodel in die Hebreërbrief," *ThEv* 15 (1982): 3-6.

0738 Erich Grässer, "Mose und Jesus: zur Auslegung von Hebr 3:1-6," *ZNW* 75 (1984): 2-23.

oaths

0739 David R. Worley, "Fleeing to Two Immutable Things, God's Oath-Taking and Oath-Witnessing: The Use of Litigant Oath in Hebrews 6:12-20," *RQ* 36 (1994): 223-36.

obedience

0740 George Duncan, "Obedience and Faith," in David Porter, ed., *The People and the King*. Bromley, England: Send the Light Trust, 1980. Pp. 122-127

0741 August Konkel, "The Sacrifice of Obedience," *Didask* 2 (1991): 2-11.

0742 Timothy M. Willis, " 'Obey Your Leaders': Hebrews 13 and Leadership in the Church," *RQ* 36 (1994): 316-26.

Parables

0743 Steve Stanley, "Hebrews 9:6-10: The 'Parable' of the Tabernacle," *NovT* 37 (1995): 385-99.

Paraenesis

0744 Wolfgang Schenk, "Die Paränese Hebr 13:16 im Kontext des Hebräerbriefs: einer Fallstudie semiotisch-orientierter Textinterpretation und Sachkritik," *StTheol* 39 (1985): 73-106.

Paul, Saint

0745 Charles P. Anderson, "The Epistle to the Hebrews and the Pauline Letter Collection," *HTR* 59 (1966): 429-38.

0746 Ulrich Luz, "Der alte und der neue Bund bei Paulus und im Hebräerbrief," *EvT* 27 (1967): 318-36.

0747 Royal Sage, "Paul the Author of Hebrews?" in Vern Carner and Gary Stanhiser, eds., *The Stature of Christ* (festschrift for Edward Heppenstall). Loma Linda CA: Carner and Stanhiser, 1970. Pp. 122-26.

0748 Friedrich Schröger, "Der Hebraeerbrief: Paulinisch?" in Paul G. Mueller and Werner Stenger, eds., *Kontinuitaet und Einheit* (festschrift for Franz Mussner). Freiburg: Herder, 1981. Pp. 211-22.

0749 Gerald L. Borchert, "A Superior Book: Hebrews," *RevExp* 82 (1985): 319-22.

0750 David G. Peterson, "The Ministry of Encouragement," in Peter T. O'Brien and David G. Peterson, eds., *God Who Is Rich in Mercy* (festschrift for D. B. Knox). Homebush, Australia: Lancer Books, 1986. Pp. 235-53.

0751 Otto Betz, "Firmness in faith: Hebrews 11:1 and Isaiah 28:16," in Barry P. Thompson, ed., *Scripture: Meaning and Method:*. (festschrift for A. T. Hanson). Hull UK: Hull University Press, 1987. Pp. 92-113.

0752 Roger T. Beckwith, "The Death of Christ as a Sacrifice in the Teaching of Paul and Hebrews," in Roger T. Beckwith and Martin J. Selman, eds., *Sacrifice in the Bible*. Grand Rapids: Baker Book House, 1995. Pp. 130-35.

perfection

0753 A. A. Ahern, "The Perfection Concept in the Epistle to the Hebrews," *JBR* 14 (1946): 164-67.

0754 A. Wikgren, "Patterns of Perfection in the Epistle to the Hebrews," *NTS* 6 (1959-1960): 159-66.

perseverance

0755 Robert A. Peterson, "The Perseverance of the Saints: A Theological Exegesis of Four Key New Testament Passages," *Pres* 17 (1991): 95-112.

0756 Thomas E. Schmidt, "Moral Lethargy and the Epistle to the Hebrews," *WTJ* 54 (1992): 167-73.

Philo

0757 Ronald H. Nash, "Notion of Mediator in Alexandrian Judaism and the Epistle to the Hebrews," *WTJ* 40 (1977): 89-115.

0758 Antonio Vicent Cernuda, "La introducción del Primogénito, según Hebr 1:6," *EB* NS 39 (1981): 107-53.

0759 William L. Lane, "Detecting Divine Wisdom in Hebrews 1:14," in John H. Skilton and Curtiss A. Ladley, eds., *The New Testament Student and His Field*. The New Testament Student #5. Phillipsburg NJ: Presbyterian and Reformed Publishing Co., 1982. Pp. 150-58.

0760 Henk Jan de Jonge, "Traditie en exegese: de hogepriester-christologie en Melchizedek in Hebreeën," *NTT* 37 (1983): 1-19.

0761 Ronald Williamson, "The Incarnation of the Logos in Hebrews," *ET* 95 (1983): 4-8.

0762 Jeffrey R. Sharp, "Philonism and the Eschatology of Hebrews: Another Look," *EAJT* 2 (1984): 289-98.

0763 Ceslaus Spicq, "L'Epître aux Hébreux et Philon: un cas d'insertion de la littérature sacrée dans la culture profane du Iuer Psiècle," in Wolfgang Haase, ed., *Principat 25, 4: Religion*. New York: Walter de Gruyter, 1987. Pp. 3602-18.

Platonists
0764 Lincoln D. Hurst, "How 'Platonic' Are Hebrews 8:5 and Hebrews 9:23f?" *JTS* NS 34 (1983): 156-68.

priesthood
0765 Olaf Moe, "Der Gedanke des allgemeinen Priestertums im Hebräerbrief," *TZ* 5 (1949): 161-69.

0766 Nils A. Dahl, "A New and Living Way: The Approach to God according to Hebrews 10:19-25," *Int* 5 (1951): 401-12.

0767 A. J. B. Higgins, "Priest and Messiah," *VT* 3 (1953): 321-36.

0768 Gottfried Schille, "Erwägungen zur Hohenpriesterlehre des Hebräerbriefes," *ZNW* 46 (1955): 81-109.

0769 William M. F. Scott, "Priesthood in the New Testament," *SJT* 10 (1957): 399-415.

0770 C. Bourgin, "Le Christ-Prêtre et la purification des péchés selon l'épître aux Hébreux," *LVie* 36 (1958): 67-90.

0771 H. Zimmerman, *Die Hohepriester -Christologic des Hebräerbriefes*. Paderborn: Schöningh, 1964.

0772 James Swetnam, "On the Imagery and Significance of Hebrews 9:9-10," *CBQ* 28 (1966): 155-73.

0773 Otto Glombitza, "Erwägungen zum kunstvollen Ansatz der Paraenese im Brief an die Hebräer 10:19-25," *NovT* 9 (1967): 132-50.

0774 R. A. Stewart, "The Sinless High-Priest," *NTS* 14 (1967-1968): 126-35.

0775 S. Nomoto, "Herkunft und Struktur der Hohenpriestervorstellung im Hebräerbrief," *NovT* 10 (1968): 10-25.

0776 Egon Brandenburger, "Text und Vorlagen von Hebr 5:7-10: ein Beitrag zur Christologie des Hebräerbriefs," *NovT* 11 (1969): 190-224.

0777 Albert Vanhoye, *Le Christ est notre prêtre: La doctrine de l'épître aux Hébreux*. Toulouse: Editions Prière et Vie, 1969.

0778 P.-É. Langevin, "Le sacerdoce du Christ dans le Nouveau Testament, surtout d'après l'épître aux Hébreux," in *Le prêtre, hier, aujourd'hui, demain*. Montréal: Fides, 1970. Pp. 63-79.

0779 Ronald Williamson, "Hebrews 4:15 and the Sinlessness of Jesus," *ET* 86 (1974): 4-8.

0780 E. A. C. Pretorius, "Christusbeeld en Kerkmodel in die Hebreërbrief," *ThEv* 15 (1982): 3-6.

0781 William Horbury, "The Aaronic Priesthood in the Epistle to the Hebrews," *JSNT* 19 (1983): 43-71.

0782 Henk Jan de Jonge, "Traditie en exegese: de hogepriester-christologie en Melchizedek in Hebreeën," *NTT* 37 (1983): 1-19.

0783 Gerald L. Borchert, "A Superior Book: Hebrews," *RevExp* 82 (1985): 319-22.

0784 Paul Ellingworth, "The Unshakable Priesthood: Hebrews 7:24," *JSNT* 23 (1985): 125-26.

0785 Wolfgang Schenk, "Die Paränese Hebr 13:16 im Kontext des Hebräerbriefs: einer Fallstudie semiotisch-orientierter Textinterpretation und Sachkritik," *StTheol* 39 (1985): 73-106.

0786 Harold S. Songer, "A Superior Priesthood: Hebrews 4:14-7:27," *RevExp* 82 (1985): 345-59.

0787 Paul Ellingworth, "Jesus and the Universe in Hebrews," *EQ* 58 (1986): 337-350.

0788 Michael Bachmann, "Hohepriesterliches Leiden: Beobachtungen zu Heb 5:1-10," *ZNW* 78 (1987): 244-66.

0789 Gabriel Josipovici, "The Epistle to the Hebrews and the Catholic Epistles," in Robert Alter and Frank Kermode, eds., *The Literary Guide to the Bible*. Cambridge MA: Harvard University Press, 1987. Pp. 503-22.

0790 Alan Mugridge, "Warnings in the Epistle to the Hebrews: An Exegetical and Theological Study," *RTR* 46 (1987): 74-82.

0791 M. J. Paul, "The Order of Melchizedek (Ps 110:4 and Heb 7:3)," *WTJ* 49 (1987): 195-211.

0792 George H. Tavard, "The Meaning of Melchizedek for Contemporary Ministry," in Earl E. Shelp and Ronald H. Sunderland, eds., *The Pastor as Priest*. New York: Pilgrim Press, 1987. Pp. 64-85.

0793 Mario Caprioli, "Il sacerdozio di Cristo," in Antonio Piolanti, ed., *Atti del IX Congresso tomistico internazionale, 6: Storia del tomismo*. Vatican City: Libreria Editrice Vaticana, 1991. Pp. 96-105.

0794 Harald Hegermann, "Christologie im Hebräerbrief," in Cilliers Breytenbach and Henning Paulsen, eds., *Anfänge der Christologie* (festschrift for Ferdinand Hahn). Göttingen: Vandenhoeck & Ruprecht, 1991. Pp. 337-51.

0795 August Konkel, "The Sacrifice of Obedience," *Didask* 2 (1991): 2-11.

0796 David J. MacLeod, "The Present Work of Christ in Hebrews," *BS* 148 (1991): 184-200.

0797   Albert Vanhoye, "Anamnèse historique et créativité théologique dans l'épître aux Hébreux," in Daniel Marguerat and Jean Zumstein, eds., *La mémoire et le temps* (festschrift for Pierre Bonnard). Le monde de la Bible #23. Geneva: Labor et Fides, 1991. Pp. 219-31.

0798   Franz Laub, "Glaubenskrise und neu auszulegendes Bekenntnis: Zur Intention der Hohepriesterchristologie des Hebräerbriefes," in Joesf Hainz, ed., *Theologie im Werden: Studien zu den theologischen Konzeptionen im Neuen Testament.* Paderborn: Ferdinand Schöningh, 1992. Pp. 377-96.

0799   Peter J. Leithart, "The Priests of Culture," *FirstT* 27 (1992): 10-12.

0800   Christopher D. Marshall, "One for All and All for One: The High Priesthood of Christ, the Church, and the Priesthood of All Believers in Hebrews," *JCBRF* 129 (1992): 7-13.

0801   Claus P. März, "Vom Trost der Theologie: Zur Pragmatik der christologisch-soteriologischen Reflexion im Hebräerbrief," in Wilhem Ernst and Konrad Feiereis, eds., *Denkender Glaube im Geschichte und Gegenwart.* Erfurter theologische Studien #63. Leipzig: Benno-Verlag, 1992. Pp. 260-76.

0802   David J. MacLeod, "The Cleansing of the True Tabernacle," *BSac* 152 (1995): 60-71.

0803   Albert Vanhoye, "La '*teleiôsis*' du Christ," *NTS* 42 (1996): 321-38.

Qumran

0804   Y. Yadin, "The Dead Sea Scrolls and the Epistle to the Hebrews," in C. Rabin and Y. Yadin, eds., *Aspects of the Dead Sea Scrolls.* Jerusalem: Magnes Press, 1958. Pp. 36-55.

0805   H. Kosmala, *Hebräer - Essener - Christen. Studien zur Vorgeschichte der frühchristlichen Verkündigung.* Leiden: Brill, 1959.

0806   Ceslaus Spicq, "L'Épître aux Hébreux, Apollos, Jean-Baptiste, les Hellénistes et Qumrān," *RevQ* 1 (1959): 365-90.

0807   J. Coppens, *Les affinités qumrāniennes de l'Épître aux Hébreux.* Paris: Desclée de Brouwer, 1962.

0808 F. F. Bruce, " 'To the Hebrews' or 'To the Essenes'?" *NTS* 9 (1962-1963): 217-32.

0809 H. Braun, "Fragen des Hebräerbriefes," in *Qumran und das Neue Testament.* Volume 2. Tübingen: Mohr, 1966. Pp. 181-84.

0810 I. W. Batdorf, "Hebrews and Qumran: Old Methods and New Directions," in E. Barth and R. Cocroft, eds., *Festschrift for F. Wilbur Gingrich.* Leiden: Brill, 1972. Pp. 16-35.

0811 Mark A. Seifrid, "Paul's Approach to the Old Testament in Romans 10:6-8," *TriJ* NS 6 (1985): 3-37.

0812 Hermut Löhr, "Thronversammlung und preisender Tempel: Beobachtungen am himmlischen Heiligtum im Hebräerbrief und in den Sabbatopferliedern aus Qumran," in Martin Hengel and Anna M. Schwemer, eds., *Königsherrschaft Gottes und himmlischer Kult im Judentum, Urchristentum und in der hellenistischen Welt.* Wissenschaftliche Untersuchungen zum Neuen Testament #55. Tübingen: Mohr, 1991. Pp. 185-205.

0813 Herbert W. Bateman, "Two First-Century Messianic Uses of the OT: Hebrews 1:5-13 and 4QFlor 1.1-19," *JETS* 38 (1995): 11-27.

Rabbinic literature

0814 Andrew T. Lincoln, "Sabbath, Rest, and Eschatology in the New Testament," in Don A. Carson, ed., *From Sabbath to Lord's Day: A Biblical, Historical and Theological Investigation.* Grand Rapids MI: Zondervan Publishing House, 1982. Pp. 198-220.

0815 Albert Vanhoye, "Héb 6:7-8 et le mashal rabbinique," in William C. Weinrich, ed., *The New Testament Age* (festschrift for Bo Reicke). 2 vols. Macon GA: Mercer Universitry Press, 1984. 1:527-32.

0816 Mark A. Seifrid, "Paul's Approach to the Old Testament in Romans 10:6-8," *TriJ* NS 6 (1985): 3-37.

Rahab

0817 William H. Willimon, "Best Little Harlot's House in Jericho," *CC* 100 (1983): 956-58.

relation to Old Testament

0818 W. Leonard, *The Authorship of the Epistle to the Hebrews: Critical Problem and Use of the Old Testament*. London: Burns Oates & Washbourne, 1939.

0819 Peter Katz, "Hebrews 13:5: The Biblical Source of the Quotation," *Bib* 33 (1952): 523-25.

0820 August Strobel, "Die Psalmengrundlage der Gethsemane-Parallele, Hebr 5:7ff," *ZNW* 45 (1954): 252-66.

0821 Peter Katz, "The Quotations from Deuteronomy in Hebrews," *ZNW* 49 (1958): 213-23.

0822 George B. Caird, "The Exegetical Method of the Epistle to Hebrews," *CJT* 5 (1959): 44-51.

0823 F. C. Synge, *Hebrews and the Scriptures*. London: S.P.C.K., 1959.

0824 Simon Kistemaker, *The Psalm Citations in the Epistle to the Hebrews*. Amsterdam: G. Van Soest, 1961.

0825 M. Barth, "The Old Testament in Hebrews. An Essay in Biblical Hermeneutics," in W. Klassen and D. Synder, eds., *Current Issues in New Testament* (festschrift for Otto Piper). London: SCM Press, 1962. Pp. 53-78.

0826 M. Barth, "Freedom Exemplified: The Use of the Old Testament in Hebrews," in *Conversation with the Bible*. New York: Holt, Rinehart and Winston, 1964. Pp. 201-35.

0827 K. J. Thomas, "The Old Testament Citations in Hebrews," *NTS* 11 (1964-1965): 303-25.

0828 Thomas F. Glasson, "Plurality of Divine Persons and the Quotations in Hebrews 1:6ff," *NTS* 12 (1966): 270-72.

0829 Hugolinus Langkammer, "Den er zum Erben von allem eingesetzt hat," *BZ* NS 10 (1966): 273-80.

0830 G. Howard, "Hebrews and the Old Testament Quotations," *NovT* 10 (1968): 208-16.

0831   Friedrich Schröger, *Der Verfasser des Hebräerbneles als Schriftausleger.* Regensburg: Pustet, 1968.

0832   Kenneth G. Hagen, "Problem of Testament in Luther's Lectures on Hebrews," *HTR* 63 (1970): 61-90.

0833   H. J. B. Combrink, "Some Thoughts on the Old Testament Citations in The Epistle to the Hebrews," *Neo* 5 (1971): 22-36.

0834   Jan Heller, "Stabesanbetung?" *CVia* 16 (1973): 257-65.

0835   K. J. Thomas, "The Old Testament Citations in Hebrews," in Sidney Jellicoe, ed., *Studies in the Septuagint.* New York: Ktav, 1974. Pp. 507-29.

0836   George MacRae, "A Kingdom that Cannot Be Shaken: The Heavenly Jerusalem in the Letter to the Hebrews," in Pierre Bonnard, et al., *Spirituality and Ecumenism.* Jerusalem: Ecumenical Institute for Theological Research, 1980. Pp. 27-40.

0837   Albert Vanhoye, "Literarische Struktur und theologische Botschaft des Hebräerbriefs," *SNTU-A* 5 (1980): 18-49.

0838   Andrew T. Lincoln, "Sabbath, Rest, and Eschatology in the New Testament," in Don A. Carson, ed., *From Sabbath to Lord's Day: A Biblical, Historical and Theological Investigation.* Grand Rapids MI: Zondervan Publishing House, 1982. Pp. 198-220.

0839   William Horbury, "The Aaronic Priesthood in the Epistle to the Hebrews," *JSNT* 19 (1983): 43-71.

0840   Jean P. Michaud, "Le passage de l'ancien au nouveau, selon l'épître aux Hébreux," *SE* 35 (1983): 33-52.

0841   Moisés Silva, "The New Testament Use of the Old Testament: Text Form and Authority," in Don A. Carson and John D. Woodbridge, eds., *Scripture and Truth.* Grand Rapids: Zondervan, 1983. Pp. 147-65.

0842   Agustín del Agua Pérez, "Procedimientos derásicos del Sal 2:7b en el Nuevo Testamento: Tu eres mi hijo, yo te he engendrado hoy," *EB* NS 42 (1984): 391-414.

0843   J. Duncan M. Derrett, "Running in Paul: The Midrashic Potential of Habakkuk 2:2," *Bib* 66 (1985): 560-67.

0844   Murray J. Harris, "The Translation and Significance of *Ho theos* in Hebrews 1:8-9," *TynB* 36 (1985): 129-62.

0845   John P. Meier, "Symmetry and Theology in the Old Testament Citations of Hebrews 1:5-14," *Bib* 66 (1985): 504-33.

0846   Mark A. Seifrid, "Paul's Approach to the Old Testament in Romans 10:6-8," *TriJ* NS 6 (1985): 3-37.

0847   Thomas G. Smothers, "A Superior Model: Hebrews 1:1-4:13," *RevExp* 82 (1985): 333-43.

0848   William Klassen, "To the Hebrews or against the Hebrews: Anti-Judaism and the Epistle to the Hebrews," in Stephen Wilson, ed., *Anti-Judaism in Early Christianity*. Volume 2: *Separation and Polemic*. Studies in Christianity and Judaism #2. Waterloo, Ontario: Wilfried Laurier University Press, 1986. Pp. 1-16.

0849   Marcus L. Loane, "The Unity of the Old and New Testaments as Illustrated in the Epistle to the Hebrews," in Peter T. O'Brien and David G. Peterson, eds., *God Who Is Rich in Mercy* (festschrift for D. B. Knox). Homebush, Australia: Lancer Books, 1986. Pp. 255-64.

0850   Paul-Gerhard Müller, "Die Funktion der Psalmzitate im Hebräerbrief," in Ernst Haag and F.-L. Hossfeld, eds., *Freude an der Weisung des Herrn: Beiträge zur Theologie der Psalmen* (festschrift for Heinrich Gross). Stuttgart: Verlag Katholisches Bibelwerk, 1986. Pp. 223-42.

0851   Otto Betz, "Firmness in faith: Hebrews 11:1 and Isaiah 28:16," in Barry P. Thompson, ed., *Scripture: Meaning and Method:*. (festschrift for A. T. Hanson). Hull UK: Hull University Press, 1987. Pp. 92-113.

0852   Stanley Frost, "Who Were the Heroes: An Exercise in Bi-testamentary Exegesis, with Christological Implications," in L. D. Hurst and Nicholas T. Wright, eds., *The Glory of Christ in the New Testament: Studies in Christology*. Oxford: Clarendon Press, 1987. Pp. 165-72.

0853   Lincoln D. Hurst, "The Christology of Hebrews 1 and 2," in L. D. Hurst and Nicholas T. Wright, eds., *The Glory of Christ in the New*

Testament: Studies in Christology. Oxford: Clarendon Press, 1987. Pp. 151-64.

0854 Gabriel Josipovici, "The Epistle to the Hebrews and the Catholic Epistles," in Robert Alter and Frank Kermode, eds., *The Literary Guide to the Bible*. Cambridge MA: Harvard University Press, 1987. Pp. 503-22.

0855 David Flusser, "Today If You Will Listen to This Voice: Creative Exegesis in Hebrews 3-4," in Benjamin Uffenheimer, et al., eds., - *Creative Biblical Exegesis: Christian and Jewish Hermeneutics through the Centuries*. Sheffield: JSOT Press, 1988. Pp. 55-62.

0856 Charles P. Anderson, "Who Are the Heirs of the New Age in the Epistle to the Hebrews?" in Joel Marcus and Marion Soards, eds., *Apocalyptic and the New Testament* (festschrift for J. Louis Martyn). Sheffield: JSOT Press, 1989. Pp. 255-77.

0857 Scott C. Layton, "Christ over His House (Hebrew 3:6) and Hebrew '*shr l-hbyt* [Gen 37-50, 1-2 Kgs]," *NTS* 37 (1991): 473-77.

0858 Alan H. Cadwallader, "The Correction of the Text of Hebrews towards the LXX," *NovT* 34 (1992): 257-92.

0859 Karen H. Jobes, "The Function of *paronomasia* in Hebrews 10:5-7," *TriJ* 13 (1992): 181-91.

0860 Franz Laub, "Glaubenskrise und neu auszulegendes Bekenntnis: Zur Intention der Hohepriesterchristologie des Hebräerbriefes," in Joesf Hainz, ed., *Theologie im Werden: Studien zu den theologischen Konzeptionen im Neuen Testament*. Paderborn: Ferdinand Schöningh, 1992. Pp. 377-96.

0861 David G. Peterson, "Biblical Theology and the Argument of Hebrews," in Peterson John Pryor, eds., *In the Fullness of Time* (festschrift for Donald Robinson). Homebush West NSW: Lancer, 1992. Pp. 219-35.

0862 Peter E. Enns, "Creation and Re-Creation: Psalm 95 and Its Interpretation in Hebrews 3:1-4:13," *WTJ* 55 (1993): 255-80.

0863   Theo C. de Kruijf, "The Priest-King Melchizedek: The Reception of Gen 14,18-20 in Hebrews Mediated by Psalm 110," *Bij* 54 (1993): 393-406.

0864   Hermut Löhr, " 'Umriss' und 'Schatten': Bemerkungen zur Zitierung von Ex 25,40 in Hebr 8," *ZNW* 84 (1993): 218-32.

0865   Mark Saucy, "Exaltation Christology in Hebrews: What Kind of Reign?" *TriJ* 14 (1993): 41-62.

0866   Otfried Hofius, "Biblische Theologie im Lichte des Hebräerbriefes," in Sigfred Pedersen, ed., *New Directions in Biblical Theology.* Leiden: Brill, 1994. Pp. 108-25.

0867   Dale F. Leschert, *Hermeneutical Foundations of Hebrews: A Study in the Validity of the Epistle's Interpretation of Some Core Citations from the Psalms.* NABPR Dissertation Series #10. Lewiston NY: Mellen Press, 1994.

0868   James Swetnam, "Hebrews 10,30-31: A Suggestion," *Bib* 75 (1994): 388-94.

0869   Herbert W. Bateman, "Two First-Century Messianic Uses of the OT: Hebrews 1:5-13 and 4QFlor 1.1-19," *JETS* 38 (1995): 11-27.

0870   G. W. Grogan, "The Old Testament Concept of Solidarity in Hebrews," *TynB* 49 (1998): 159-73.

rest

0871   Andrew T. Lincoln, "Sabbath, Rest, and Eschatology in the New Testament," in Don A. Carson, ed., *From Sabbath to Lord's Day: A Biblical, Historical and Theological Investigation.* Grand Rapids MI: Zondervan Publishing House, 1982. Pp. 198-220.

0872   Khiok-Khng Yeo, "The Meaning and Usage of the Theology of 'Rest' in Hebrews 3:7-4:13," *AsiaJT* 5 (1991): 2-33.

0873   Jon Laansma, *"I Will Give You Rest": The Rest Motif in the New Testament with Special Reference to Matthew 11 and Hebrews 3-4.* Tübingen: Mohr, 1997.

resurrection
> **0874** Luis F. Ladaria, "Presente y futuro en la escatología cristiana," *EE* 60 (1985): 351-59.

rhetoric
> **0875** David Alan Black, "Hebrews 1:1-4: A Study in Discourse Analysis," *WTJ* 49 (1987): 175-94.

> **0876** Seán Freyne, "Reading Hebrews and Revelation Intertextually," in Spike Draisma, ed., *Intertextuality in Biblical Writings* (festschrift for Bas van Iersel). Kampen: J. H. Kok, 1989. Pp. 83-93.

> **0877** Karen H. Jobes, "The Function of *paronomasia* in Hebrews 10:5-7," *TriJ* 13 (1992): 181-91.

> **0878** Alan C. Mitchell, "The Use of *prepein* and Rhetorical Propriety in Hebrews 2:10," *CBQ* 54 (1992): 681-701.

> **0879** Thomas H. Olbricht, "Hebrews as Amplification," in Stanley E. Porter, and Thomas H. lbricht, eds., *Rhetoric and the New Testament.* Sheffield UK: JSOT Press, 1993. Pp. 375-87.

> **0880** Steve Stanley, "The Structure of Hebrews from Three Perspectives," *TynB* 45 (1994): 245-71.

> **0881** David R. Worley, "Fleeing to Two Immutable Things, God's Oath-Taking and Oath-Witnessing: The Use of Litigant Oath in Hebrews 6:12-20," *RQ* 36 (1994): 223-36.

> **0882** David A. DeSilva, *Despising Shame: Honor Discourse and Community Maintenance in the Epistle to the Hebrews.* Atlanta: Scholars Press, 1995.

> **0883** Alan D. Bulley, "Death and Rhetoric in the Hebrews 'Hymn to Faith'," *SR* 25 (1996): 409-23.

sabbath
> **0884** Roy Graham, "A Note on Hebrews 4:4-9," in Kenneth A. Strand, ed., *The Sabbath in Scripture and History.* Washington: Review and Herald Publication Association, 1982. Pp. 343-45.

sacrifice

0885   James Swetnam, "Sacrifice and Revelation in the Epistle to the Hebrews: Observations and Surmises on Hebrews 9:26," *CBQ* 30 (1968): 227-34.

0886   Ortensio Da Spinetoli, "Il senso della croce nella lettera agli Ebrei: portata storica e interpretazione teologica," in Christian Duquoc, et al., eds., *La sapienza della croce oggi, 1: la sapienza della croce nella rivelazione e nell'ecumenismo.* Turin: Elle Di Ci, 1976. Pp. 136-43.

0887   Albert Vanhoye, "Esprit éternel et feu du sacrifice en He 9:14," *Bib* 64 (1983): 263-274.

0888   Rinaldo Fabris, "La morte di Gesù nella lettera agli Ebrei," in Giovanni Boggio, et al., *Gesù e la sua morte.* Brescia: Paideia Editrice, 1984. Pp. 177-89.

0889   Roger L. Omanson, "A Superior Covenant: Hebrews 8:1-10:18," *RevExp* 82 (1985): 361-73.

0890   Armando J. Levoratti, "Tú no has querido sacrificio ni oblación: Salmo 40:7; Hebreos 10:5; pt 2," *RevB* 48 (1986): 193-237.

0891   Nello Casalini, "I sacrifici dell'antica alleanza nel piano salvifico di Dio secondo la lettera agli Ebrei," *RivBib* 35 (1987): 443-64.

0892   A. N. Chester, "Hebrews: The Final Sacrifice," in Stephen W. Sykes, ed., *Sacrifice and Redemption: Durham Essays in Theology.* Cambridge: University Press, 1991. Pp. 57-72.

0893   Barnabas Lindars, "Hebrews and the Second Temple," in William Horbury, ed., *Templum Amicitiae: Essays on the Second Temple* (festschrift for Ernst Bammel). Sheffield: JSOT Press, 1991. Pp. 410-33.

0894   John Dunnill, *Covenant and Sacrifice in the Letter to the Hebrews.* Cambridge: University Press, 1992.

0895   Gerd Schunack, "Jesu 'Opfertod' im Hebräerbrief," in Ulrich Schoenborn and Stephan Pfürtner, eds., *Der bezwingende Vorsprung des Guten: exegetische und theologische Werkstattberichte* (festschrift for Wolfgang Harnisch). Munster: Lit, 1994. Pp. 209-31.

Sarah
   0896   Pieter W. van der Horst, "Did Sarah Have a Seminal Emission?" *BRev*
             8 (1992): 35-39.

second Adam
   0897   Robert W. Thurston, "Philo and the Epistle to the Hebrews," *EQ* 58
             (1986): 133-43.

semiotics
   0898   Wolfgang Schenk, "Die Paränese Hebr 13:16 im Kontext des
             Hebräerbriefs: einer   Fallstudie   semiotisch-orientierter
             Textinterpretation und Sachkritik," *StTheol* 39 (1985): 73-106.

Septuagint
   0899   Moisés Silva, "The New Testament Use of the Old Testament: Text
             Form and Authority," in Don A. Carson and John D. Woodbridge,
             eds., *Scripture and Truth*. Grand Rapids: Zondervan, 1983. Pp.
             147-65.

   0900   Alan H. Cadwallader, "The Correction of the Text of Hebrews
             towards the LXX," *NovT* 34 (1992): 257-92.

sinlessness
   0901   Bernhard Heininger, "Sündenreinigung (Hebr 1,3): Christologie
             Anmerkungen zum Exordium des Hebräerbriefs," *BZ* NS 41 (1997):
             54-68.

sociology
   0902   David A. DeSilva, "Despising Shame: A Cultural-Anthropological
             Investigation of the Epistle to the Hebrews," *JBL* 113 (1994): 439-61.

Son of God
   0903   Edvin Larsson, "Sonen och änglarna i Hebr 1-2," in Ivar Asheim, et
             al., eds., *Israel, Kristus, kirken* (festschrift for Sverre Aalen). Oslo:
             Universitetsforlaget, 1979. Pp. 91-108.

   0904   Paul Ellingworth, "Like the Son of God: Form and Content in
             Hebrews 7:1-10," *Bib* 64 (1983): 255-262.

   0905   George B. Caird, "Son by Appointment," in William C. Weinrich, ed.,
             The New Testament Age (festschrift for Bo Reicke). 2 vols. Macon
             GA: Mercer Universitry Press, 1984. 1:73-81.

0906 Peter R. Jones, "A Superior Life: Hebrews 12:3-13:25," *RevExp* 82 (1985): 391-405.

0907 Harald Hegermann, "Christologie im Hebräerbrief," in Cilliers Breytenbach and Henning Paulsen, eds., *Anfänge der Christologie* (festschrift for Ferdinand Hahn). Göttingen: Vandenhoeck & Ruprecht, 1991. Pp. 337-51.

0908 Kenneth Schenck, "Keeping His Appointment: Creation and Enthronement in Hebrews," *JSNT* 66 (1997): 91-117.

soteriology

0909 Nils A. Dahl, "A New and Living Way: The Approach to God according to Hebrews 10:19-25," *Int* 5 (1951): 401-12.

0910 Mark R. Shaw, "Is There Salvation outside the Christian Faith," *EAJT* 2 (1983): 42-62.

0911 Rinaldo Fabris, "La morte di Gesù nella lettera agli Ebrei," in Giovanni Boggio, et al., *Gesù e la sua morte.* Brescia: Paideia Editrice, 1984. Pp. 177-89.

0912 Ronald Sauer, "Can Salvation Be Lost," *FundJ* 3 (1984): 54.

0913 C. Samuel Storms, "Defining the Elect," *JETS* 27 (1984): 205-18.

0914 Charles R. Smith, "The Book of Life," *GTJ* 6 (1985): 219-30.

0915 Julius J. Scott, "Archegos: The Salvation History of the Epistle to the Hebrews," *JETS* 29 (1986): 47-54.

0916 Nello Casalini, "I sacrifici dell'antica alleanza nel piano salvifico di Dio secondo la lettera agli Ebrei," *RivBib* 35 (1987): 443-64.

0917 Alan Mugridge, "Warnings in the Epistle to the Hebrews: An Exegetical and Theological Study," *RTR* 46 (1987): 74-82.

0918 Claus P. März, "Vom Trost der Theologie: Zur Pragmatik der christologisch-soteriologischen Reflexion im Hebräerbrief," in Wilhem Ernst and Konrad Feiereis, eds., *Denkender Glaube im Geschichte und Gegenwart.* Erfurter theologische Studien #63. Leipzig: Benno-Verlag, 1992. Pp. 260-76.

0919   Scot McKnight, "The Warning Passages of Hebrews: A Formal Analysis and Theological Conclusions," *TriJ* 13 (1992): 21-59.

0920   Wayne R. Kempson, "Hebrews 6:1-8," *RevExp* 91 (1994): 567-73.

0921   Brenda B. Colijn, " 'Let Us Approach': Soteriology in the Epistle to the Hebrews," *JETS* 39 (1996): 571-86.

Stoics

0922   David E. Aune, "Heracles and Christ: Heracles Imagery in the Christology of Early Christianity," in David L. Balch, et als., eds., *Greeks, Romans, and Christians* (festschrift for Abraham J. Malherbe. Minneapolis: Fortress Press, 1990. Pp. 3-19.

structuralism

0923   Daniel J. Ebert, "The Chiastic Structure of the Prologue to Hebrews," *TriJ* 13 (1992): 163-79.

suffering

0924   Alan D. Bulley, "Death and Rhetoric in the Hebrews 'Hymn to Faith'," *SR* 25 (1996): 409-23.

symbolism

0925   George H. Tavard, "The Meaning of Melchizedek for Contemporary Ministry," in Earl E. Shelp and Ronald H. Sunderland, eds., *The Pastor as Priest*. New York: Pilgrim Press, 1987. Pp. 64-85.

tabernacle

0926   Roger L. Omanson, "A Superior Covenant: Hebrews 8:1-10:18," *RevExp* 82 (1985): 361-73.

0927   Steve Stanley, "Hebrews 9:6-10: The 'Parable' of the Tabernacle," *NovT* 37 (1995): 385-99.

textual criticism

0928   R. V. G. Tasker, "The Integrity of the Epistle to the Hebrews," *ET* 47 (1935-1936): 136-38.

0929   F. W. Beare, "The Text of the Epistle to the Hebrews in P46," *JBL* 63 (1944): 379-96.

0930   Jose M. Bover, "Las variante mellonton y genomenon en Hebrews 9:11," *Bib* 32 (1951): 232-36.

0931   Alberto Vaccari, "Hebr 12,1: lectio emendatior," *Bib* 39 (1958): 471-77.

0932   Albert Vanhoye, "Discussions sur la structure de l'Épître aux Hébreux," *Bib* 55 (1974): 349-80.

0933   Moisés Silva, "The New Testament Use of the Old Testament: Text Form and Authority," in Don A. Carson and John D. Woodbridge, eds., *Scripture and Truth*. Grand Rapids: Zondervan, 1983. Pp. 147-65.

0934   Johannes L. P. Wolmarans, "The Text and Translation of Hebrews 8:8," *ZNW* 75 (1984): 139-44.

0935   Paul Garnet, "Hebrews 2:9: Chriti or Choris," *StudPat* 18 (1985): 321-25.

0936   Reinhard F. Schlossnikel, *Der Brief an die Hebräer und das corpus Paulinum: eine linguistische 'Bruchstelle' im codex Claromontanus*. Freiburg: Herder, 1991.

0937   F. F. Bruce, "Textual Problems in the Epistle to the Hebrews," in David A. Black, ed., *Scribes and Scripture* (festschrift for J. Harold Greenlee). Winona Lake IN: Eisenbrauns, 1992. Pp. 27-39.

0938   Alan H. Cadwallader, "The Correction of the Text of Hebrews towards the LXX," *NovT* 34 (1992): 257-92.

0939   T. J. Finney, "A Proposed Reconstruction of Hebrews 7:28a in p46," *NTS* 40 (1994): 472-473.

0940   Charles W. Hedrick, "A New Coptic Fragment of the Book of Hebrews," in Jospeh E. Coleson and Victor H. Matthews, eds., *"Go to the Land I Will Show You"* (festschrift for Dwight W. Young). Winona Lake IN: Eisenbrauns, 1996. Pp. 243-46.

throne of God

0941   Hermut Löhr, "Thronversammlung und preisender Tempel: Beobachtungen am himmlischen Heiligtum im Hebräerbrief und in den Sabbatopferliedern aus Qumran," in Martin Hengel and Anna M. Schwemer, eds., *Königsherrschaft Gottes und himmlischer Kult im Judentum, Urchristentum und in der hellenistischen Welt.*

Wissenschaftliche Untersuchungen zum Neuen Testament #55. Tübingen: Mohr, 1991. Pp. 185-205.

time

0942   François Marty, "Le péché sans rémission dans l'epître aux Hébreux," in Michel Perrin, ed., *Le pardon: actes du colloque organisé par le Centre histoire des idées Université de Picardie*. Le Point théologique #45. Paris: Beauchesne, 1987. Pp. 29-47.

traditions criticism

0943   Theo C. de Kruijf, "The Priest-King Melchizedek: The Reception of Gen 14,18-20 in Hebrews Mediated by Psalm 110," *Bij* 54 (1993): 393-406.

typology

0944   Ortensio Da Spinetoli, "Il senso della croce nella lettera agli Ebrei: portata storica e interpretazione teologica," in Christian Duquoc, et al., eds., *La sapienza della croce oggi, 1: la sapienza della croce nella rivelazione e nell'ecumenismo*. Turin: Elle Di Ci, 1976. Pp. 136-43.

0945   E. A. C. Pretorius, "Christusbeeld en Kerkmodel in die Hebreërbrief," *ThEv* 15 (1982): 3-6.

0946   Jean P. Michaud, "Le passage de l'ancien au nouveau, selon l'épître aux Hébreux," *SE* 35 (1983): 33-52.

0947   Erich Grässer, "Mose und Jesus: zur Auslegung von Hebr 3:1-6," *ZNW* 75 (1984): 2-23.

0948   R. Alan Culpepper, "A Superior Faith: Hebrews 10:19-12:2," *RevExp* 82 (1985): 375-90.

0949   Thomas G. Smothers, "A Superior Model: Hebrews 1:1-4:13," *RevExp* 82 (1985): 333-43.

0950   Paul Ellingworth, "Jesus and the Universe in Hebrews," *EQ* 58 (1986): 337-350.

0951   Brian E. Colless, "The Letter to the Hebrews and the Song of the Pearl," *AbrN* 25 (1987): 40-55.

versions
> **0952** Henk Jan de Jonge, "The Character of Erasmus' Translation of the New Testament as Reflected in His Translation of Hebrews 9," *JMRS* 14 (1984): 81-87.

> **0953** Charles W. Hedrick, "A New Coptic Fragment of the Book of Hebrews," in Jospeh E. Coleson and Victor H. Matthews, eds., *"Go to the Land I Will Show You"* (festschrift for Dwight W. Young). Winona Lake IN: Eisenbrauns, 1996. Pp. 243-46.

wisdom
> **0954** Ronald H. Nash, "Notion of Mediator in Alexandrian Judaism and the Epistle to the Hebrews," *WTJ* 40 (1977): 89-115.

> **0955** William L. Lane, "Detecting Divine Wisdom in Hebrews 1:14," in John H. Skilton and Curtiss A. Ladley, eds., *The New Testament Student and His Field.* The New Testament Student #5. Phillipsburg NJ: Presbyterian and Reformed Publishing Co., 1982. Pp. 150-58.

> **0956** Kenneth Schenck, "Keeping His Appointment: Creation and Enthronement in Hebrews," *JSNT* 66 (1997): 91-117.

word studies
> **0957** Ceslaus Spicq, *"Agkyra* et *Prodromos* dans Hébr 6:19-20," *StTheol* 3 (1951): 185-87.

> **0958** Ceslaus Spicq, "Alexandrinismes dans l'Epître aux Hébreux," *RB* 58 (1951): 481-502.

> **0959** Ceslaus Spicq, "La Panégyrie de Hebr 12:22," *StTheol* 6 (1952): 30-38.

> **0960** Huw P. Owen, "The 'Stages of Ascent' in Hebrews 5:11-6:3," *NTS* 3 (1956): 243-53.

> **0961** T. C. G. Thornton, "Meaning of *ahimatekchysia* in Hebrews 9:22," *JTS* NS 15 (1964): 63-65.

> **0962** Hugolinus Langkammer, "Den er zum Erben von allem eingesetzt hat," *BZ* NS 10 (1966): 273-80.

> **0963** James Swetnam, "On the Imagery and Significance of Hebrews 9:9-10," *CBQ* 28 (1966): 155-73.

0964   J. Clifford Adams, "Exegesis of Hebrews 6:1f," *NTS* 13 (1967):
           378-85.

0965   Otto Glombitza, "Erwägungen zum kunstvollen Ansatz der Paraenese
           im Brief an die Hebräer 10:19-25," *NovT* 9 (1967): 132-50.

0966   W. L. Lorimer, "Hebrews 7:23f," *NTS* 13 (1967): 386-87.

0967   Egon Brandenburger, "Text und Vorlagen von Hebr 5:7-10: ein
           Beitrag zur Christologie des Hebräerbriefs," *NovT* 11 (1969):
           190-224.

0968   Joachim Jeremias, "Hebrér 10:20: tout' estin tes sarkos autou," *ZNW*
           62 (1971): 131.

0969   W. S. Vorster, "The Meaning of *parrēsia* in the Epistle to the
           Hebrews," *Neo* 5 (1971): 51-59.

0970   James K. Elliott, "When Jesus Was Apart from God: An Examination
           of Hebrews 2:9," *ET* 83 (1972): 339-41.

0971   L. Paul Trudinger, "*Kai gar dia bracheon epesteila Hymin*: A Note
           on Hebrews 13:22," *JTS* NS 23 (1972): 128-30.

0972   Norman H. Young, "*Tout' estin tes sarkos autou*: Apposition,
           Dependent or Explicative?" *NTS* 20 (1973): 100-104.

0973   Ronald Williamson, "Hebrews 4:15 and the Sinlessness of Jesus," *ET*
           86 (1974): 4-8.

0974   Andrew T. Lincoln, "Sabbath, Rest, and Eschatology in the New
           Testament," in Don A. Carson, ed., *From Sabbath to Lord's Day: A
           Biblical, Historical and Theological Investigation*. Grand Rapids MI:
           Zondervan Publishing House, 1982. Pp. 198-220.

0975   John D. Madden, "The Authenticity of Early Definitions of Will," in
           Felix Heinzer and Chris Schönborn, eds., *Maximus Confessor*.
           Fribourg: Editions Universitaires, 1982. Pp. 61-79.

0976   Janusz Frankowski, "Early Christian Hymns Recorded in the New
           Testament: A Reconsideration of the Question in the Light of
           Hebrews 1:3," *BZ* NS 27 (1983): 183-94.

0977   Lincoln D. Hurst, "How 'Platonic' Are Hebrews 8:5 and Hebrews 9:23f?" *JTS* NS 34 (1983): 156-68.

0978   Richard D. Patterson, "Christian Patience," *FundJ* 3 (1984): 66.

0979   David G. Peterson, "Towards a New Testament Theology of Worship," *RTR* 43 (1984): 65-73.

0980   Jarl H. Ulrichsen, "*Diaphoroteron onoma* in Hebr 1:4: Christus als Träger des Gottesnamens," *StTheol* 38 (1984): 65-75.

0981   Johannes L. P. Wolmarans, "The Text and Translation of Hebrews 8:8," *ZNW* 75 (1984): 139-44.

0982   J. Duncan M. Derrett, "Running in Paul: The Midrashic Potential of Habakkuk 2:2," *Bib* 66 (1985): 560-67.

0983   Paul Ellingworth, "The Unshakable Priesthood: Hebrews 7:24," *JSNT* 23 (1985): 125-26.

0984   Rolf Gögler, "Inkarnationsglaube und Bibeltheologie bei Origenes," *TQ* 165 (1985): 82-94.

0985   Murray J. Harris, "The Translation and Significance of *Ho theos* in Hebrews 1:8-9," *TynB* 36 (1985): 129-62.

0986   John P. Meier, "Symmetry and Theology in the Old Testament Citations of Hebrews 1:5-14," *Bib* 66 (1985): 504-33.

0987   Harold S. Camacho, "The Altar of Incense in Hebrews 9:3-4," *AUSS* 24 (1986): 5-12.

0988   Mark Kiley, "Melchisedek's Promotion to Archiereus and the Translation of *ta stoicheia tes arches*," *SBLSP* 25 (1986): 236-45.

0989   David G. Peterson, "The Ministry of Encouragement," in Peter T. O'Brien and David G. Peterson, eds., *God Who Is Rich in Mercy* (festschrift for D. B. Knox). Homebush, Australia: Lancer Books, 1986. Pp. 235-53.

0990   Julius J. Scott, "Archegos: The Salvation History of the Epistle to the Hebrews," *JETS* 29 (1986): 47-54.

0991 Gary S. Selby, "The Meaning and Function of *syneidesis* in Hebrews 9 and 10," *RQ* 28 (1986): 145-54.

0992 A. Boyd Luter, "Worship as Service: The New Testament Usage of *latreuo*," *CTR* 2 (1988): 335-44.

0993 Scott C. Layton, "Christ over His House (Hebrew 3:6) and Hebrew *'shr l-hbyt* [Gen 37-50, 1-2 Kgs]," *NTS* 37 (1991): 473-77.

0994 Jerome H. Neyrey, "Without Beginning of Days or End of Life (Hebrews 7:3): Topos for a True Deity," *CBQ* 53 (1991): 439-55.

0995 Khiok-Khng Yeo, "The Meaning and Usage of the Theology of 'Rest' in Hebrews 3:7-4:13," *AsiaJT* 5 (1991): 2-33.

0996 Pieter W. van der Horst, "Did Sarah Have a Seminal Emission?" *BRev* 8 (1992): 35-39.

0997 Karen H. Jobes, "The Function of *paronomasia* in Hebrews 10:5-7," *TriJ* 13 (1992): 181-91.

0998 Alan C. Mitchell, "The Use of *prepein* and Rhetorical Propriety in Hebrews 2:10," *CBQ* 54 (1992): 681-701.

0999 Karl Gustav E. Dolfe, "Hebrews 2,16 under the Magnifying Glass," *ZNW* 84 (1993): 289-94.

1000 Albert Vanhoye, "La *'teleiôsis'* du Christ," *NTS* 42 (1996): 321-38.

1001 John A. L. Lee, "Hebrews 5:14 and Exis: A History of Misunderstanding," *NovT* 39 (1997): 151-76.

worship
1002 David G. Peterson, "Towards a New Testament Theology of Worship," *RTR* 43 (1984): 65-73.

1003 David G. Peterson, "Further Reflections on Worship in the New Testament," *RTR* 44 (1985): 34-41.

1004 Darrell Pursiful, *The Cultic Motif in the Spirituality of the Book of Hebrews.* Lewiston NY: Mellen Biblical Press, 1993.

1005   A. Craig Troxel, " 'Cleansed Once for All': John Owen on the Glory of Gospel Worship in 'Hebrews'," *CTJ* 32 (1997): 468-79.

PART THREE

Commentaries

1006   F. W. Farrar, *The Epistle of Paul the Apostle to the Hebrews*. Cambridge: University Press, 1902.

1007   Adolph Saphir, *The Epistle to the Hebrews: An Exposition*. New York: Gospel Publishing House, 1902.

1008   William P. Dubose, *High Priesthood and Sacrifice: An Exposition of the Epistle to the Hebrews*. New York: Longmans, Green, 1908.

1009   E. J. Goodspeed, *The Epistle to the Hebrews*. New York: Macmillan, 1908.

1010   Bernhard Weiss, *Der Hebräerbrief in zeitgeschichtlicher beleuchtung*. Texte und Untersuchungen zur Geschichte der altchristlichen Literatur #35. Leipzig: Hinrichs, 1910.

1011   Alexander F. Mitchell, *Hebrews and the General Epistles: With Introduction and Notes*. New York: Revell, 1911.

1012   Alfred Seeberg, *Der briefe an die Hebräer*. Evangelisch-Theologische Bibliothek. Leipzig: Quelle and Meyer, 1912.

1013   B. H. Carroll, *Colossians, Ephesians and Hebrews*. New York: Revell, 1917.

1014   Julius Graf, *Der Hebräerbrief: Wissenschaftlich-praktische Erklärung*. Freiburg: Herder, 1918.

1015   Hugh T. Kerr, *The Supreme Gospel: A Study of the Epistle to the Hebrews*. New York: The Womans Press, 1918.

1016   S. J. Porter, *The Epistle to the Hebrews*. Nashville: Sunday School Board, Southern Baptist Convention, 1919.

1017   A. Nairne, *The Epistle to the Hebrews in the Revised Version: With Introduction and Notes*. Cambridge Bible for Schools and Colleges. Cambridge: University Press, 1921.

1018   Eduard Riggenbach, *Der Brief an die Hebräer*. Wuppertal: Brockhaus, 1922.

1019   James Moffatt, *A Critical and Exegetical Commentary on the Epistle to the Hebrews*. ICC #40. Edinburgh: T. & T. Clark, 1924.

1020   Andrew Murray, *The Holiest of All: An Exposition of the Epistle to the Hebrews*. New York: Revell, 1924.

1021   Theodor Häring, *Der briefe an die Hebräer*. Stuttgart: Calwer, 1925.

1022   J. F. McFadyen, *Through Eternal Spirit: A Study of Hebrews, James, and 1 Peter*. New York: Doran, 1925.

1023   F. D. V. Narborough, *The Epistle to the Hebrews, in the Revised Version, with Introduction and Commentary*. Oxford: The Clarendon press, 1930.

1024   Hans Windisch, *Der Hebräerbrief*. 2nd ed. HNT #14. Tübingen: Mohr, 1931.

1025   Theodore H. Robinson, *The Epistle to the Hebrews*. The Moffatt New Testament Commentary. New York: Harper, 1933.

1026   G. Campbell Morgan, *God's Last Word to Man: Studies in Hebrews*. New York: Revell, 1936.

1027   James T. Hudson, *The Epistle to the Hebrews: Its Meaning and Message*. Edinburgh: T. & T. Clark, l937.

1028   Walter D. Kallenbach, *The Message and Authorship of the Epistle to the Hebrews*. St. Paul MN: Northland Publishing House, 1938.

1029   Alexander Maclaren, *Second Timothy, Titus, Philemon and Hebrews: Hebrews, Epistle of James*. Grand Rapids MI: Eerdmans, 1944.

1030   R. C. H. Lenski, *The Interpretation of the Epistle to the Hebrews and of the Epistle of James*. Columbus OH: Wartburg Press, 1946.

1031   Peter Ketter, *Hebräerbrief, Jakobusbrief, Petrusbrief, Judasbrief*. Die Heilige Schrift für das Leben erklärt #16. Freiburg: Herder, 1950.

1032   F. B. Meyer, *The Way into the Holiest: Expositions of the Epistle to the Hebrews*. Grand Rapids: Zondervan, 1950.

1033   Adolf Schlatter, *Die Briefe des Petrus, Judas, Jakcobus, der Brief an die Hebräer*. Stuttgart: Calwer, 1950.

1034   W. F. Westcott, *The Epistle to the Hebrews: The Greek Text with Notes and Essays*. Grand Rapids: Eerdmans, 1950.

1035   P. Teodorico, *L'Epistola agli Ebrei*. La Sacra Bibbia. Torino: Marietti, 1952.

1036   Joachim Jeremias and Hermann Strathmann, *Die Briefie an Timotheus and Titus. Der Brief an die Hebräer*. Göttingen: Vandenhoeck & Ruprecht, 1953.

1037 Otto Kuss and J. Michl, *Der Brief an die Hebräer und die katholischen Briefe*. Das Neue Testament #8. Regensburg: Pustet, 1953.

1038 Hermann Strathmann, *Der Brief an die Hebräer*. Göttingen: Vandenhoeck & Ruprecht, 1954.

1039 E. Schuyler English, *Studies in the Epistle to the Hebrews*. Travelers Rest SC: Southern Bible House, 1955.

1040 William Neil, *The Epistle to the Hebrews: Introduction and Commentary*. Torch Bible Commentaries. London: SCM Press, 1955.

1041 Johannes Schneider, *The Letter to the Hebrews*. Trans. William A. Mueller. Grand Rapids: Eerdmans, 1957.

1042 Thomas Hewitt, *The Epistle to the Hebrews: An Introduction and Commentary*. The Tyndale New Testament Commentaries. Grand Rapids: Eerdmans, 1960.

1043 Thomas Hewitt, *The Epistle to the Hebrews: An Introduction and Commentary*. The Tyndale New Testament Commentaries. Grand Rapids: Eerdmans, 1960.

1044 Ernst Käsemann, *Das Wandernde Gottesvolk; eine Untersuchung zum Hebräerbrief*. 4th ed. Forschungen zur Religion und Literatur des Alten und Neuen Testaments #55. Göttingen: Vandenhoeck & Ruprecht, 1961.

1045 John W. Bowman, *The Letter to the Hebrews; the Letter of James; the First and Second Letters of Peter*. Richmond VA: John Knox Press, 1962.

1046 *Quelques notes sur l'Épître aux Hébreux*. Vevey: Éditions Bibles et traités chrétiens, 1962.

1047 F. F. Bruce, *The Epistle to the Hebrews*. Grand Rapids: Eerdmans, 1964.

1048 Hugh Montefiore, *A Commentary on the Epistle to the Hebrews*. Harper's New Testament Commentaries. New York: Harper & Row, 1964.

1049 Charles R. Erdman, *The Epistle to the Hebrews: An Exposition*. Philadelphia: Westminster Press, 1966.

1050 Otto Michel, *Der Brief an die Hebräer*. *Übersetzt und erklärt*. 12th ed. Göttingen: Vandenhoeck & Ruprecht, 1966.

1051   Albert Vanhoye, *De Epistola ad Hebraeos; sectio centralis (Cap. 8-9).*
           Rome: Pontificio Instituto Biblico, 1966.

1052   John H. Davies, *A Letter to Hebrews.* Cambridge Bible Commentary.
           Cambridge: University Press, 1967.

1053   Floyd V. Filson, *"Yesterday": A Study of Hebrews in the Light of Chapter
           13.* Studies in Biblical Theology #4. Naperville IL: A. R. Allenson, 1967.

1054   F. Laubach, *Der Brief an die Hebräer.* Wuppertal: Brockhaus, 1967.

1055   Margaret Avery, *Romans, 1 and 2 Corinthians, Galatians and Hebrews..*
           London: A.R. Mowbray, 1968.

1056   Martin Kähler, *Neutestamentliche Schriften. In genauer Wiedergabe ihres
           Gedankenganges dargestellt und durch sie selbst ausgelegt.* Darmstadt,
           Wissenschaftliche Buchgessellschaft, 1968.

1057   F. J. Schierse, *The Epistle to the Hebrews.* Trans. Benen Fahy. New
           Testament for Spiritual Reading #21. London: Burns & Oates, 1969.

1058   Jean Héring, *The Epistle to the Hebrews.* Trans. A. W. Heathcote and P. J.
           Allcock. London; Epworth Press, 1970.

1059   Geoffrey B. Wilson, *Hebrews: A Digest of Reformed Comment.* London:
           Banner of Truth Trust, 1970.

1060   Herschel H. Hobbs, *Hebrews: Challenges to Bold Discipleship.* Nashville:
           Broadman Press, 1971.

1061   James Thompson, *The Letter to the Hebrews.* Living Word Commentary #15.
           Austin TX: R. B. Sweet, 1971.

1062   John Brown, *The Epistle to the Hebrews.* London: Banner of Truth Trust,
           1972.

1063   George W. Buchanan, *To the Hebrews: Translation, Comment, and
           Conclusions.* Anchor Bible #36. Garden City NY: Doubleday, 1972.

1064   Homer A. Kent, *The Epistle to the Hebrews: A Commentary.* Grand Rapids:
           Baker Book House, 1972.

1065 Edward Fudge, *Our Man in Heaven: An Exposition of the Epistle to the Hebrews*. Grand Rapids: Baker Book House 1974.

1066 Joachim Jeremias and August Strobel, *Die Briefe an Timotheus und Titus. Der Brief an die Hebräer*. NTD #9. Göttingen: Vandenhoeck & Ruprecht, 1975.

1067 William Barclay, *The Letter to the Hebrews: Translated with an Introduction and Interpretation*. Daily Study Bible. Rev. ed. Philadelphia: Westminster, 1976.

1068 N. R. Lightfoot, *Jesus Christ Today: A Commentary on the Book of Hebrews*. Grand Rapids: Baker, 1976.

1069 Philip E. Hughes, *A Commentary on the Epistle to the Hebrews*. Grand Rapids: Eerdmans, 1977.

1070 Ceslaus Spicq, *L'épître aux Hébreux*. Sources bibliques. Paris: Gabalda, 1977.

1071 Juliana Casey, *Hebrews*. New Testament message #18. Wilmington DL: Glazier, 1980.

1072 Frederick W. Danker, *Invitation to the New Testament Epistles IV: A Commentary on Hebrews, James, 1 and 2 Peter, 1, 2, and 3 John, and Jude, with Complete Text from the Jerusalem Bible*. Doubleday New Testament Commentary Series. Garden City NY:

1073 William Gouge, *Commentary on Hebrews*. Grand Rapids: Kregel Publications, 1980.

1074 Robert Jewett, *Letter to Pilgrims: A Commentary on the Epistle to the Hebrews*. New York: Pilgrim Press, 1981.

1075 Raymond Brown, *Christ above All: The Message of Hebrews*. Downers Grove IL: InterVarsity Press, 1982.

1076 Thomas C. Edwards, *The Epistle to the Hebrews*. Minneapolis: Klock & Klock Christian Publishers, 1982.

1077 Paul Ellingworth, *A Translator's Handbook on the Letter to the Hebrews*. New York: United Bible Societies, 1983.

1078   Donald Guthrie, *The Letter to the Hebrews: An Introduction and Commentary*. Grand Rapids: Eerdmans, 1983.

1079   Donald A. Hagner, *Hebrews*. A Good News Commentary. San Francisco: Harper & Row, 1983.

1080   Norbert Hugedé, *Le sacerdoce du fils: commentaire de l'Epître aux Hébreux*. Paris: Editions Fischbacher, 1983.

1081   John MacArthur, *Hebrews / John*. Chicago: Moody Press, 1983.

1082   George MacRae, *Hebrews*. Collegeville MN: Liturgical Press, 1983.

1083   Leon Morris, *Hebrews : Bible Study Commentary*. Grand Rapids: Zondervan, 1983.

1084   Warren Quanbeck, *Revelation and the General Epistles: A Commentary on Hebrews, James, I & II Peter, I, II, and III John, Jude, Revelation*. Ed. Charles M. Laymon. Nashville: Abingdon Press, 1983.

1085   H. Braun, *An die Hebräer*. Tübingen: Mohr, 1984.

1086   Robert G. Grom, *Stand Bold in Grace: An Exposition of Hebrews*. Grand Rapids: Baker Book House, 1984.

1087   Simon Kistemaker, *Eposition of the Epistle to the Hebrews*. Grand Rapids: Baker Book House, 1984.

1088   Robert H. Smith, *Hebrews*. Minneapolis MN: Augsburg Publishing House, 1984.

1089   R. Paul Caudill, *Hebrews: A Translation with Notes*. Nashville: Broadman Press, 1985.

1090   Helmut Feld, *Der Hebräerbrief*. Darmstadt: Wissenschaftliche Buchgesellschaft, 1985.

1091   Rea McDonnell, *The Catholic Epistles and Hebrews*. Wilmington DE: Michael Glazier, 1986.

1092   Robert McL. Wilson, *Hebrews*. Grand Rapids: Eerdmans, 1987.

1093 Harald Hegermann, *Der Brief an die Hebräer*. THNT #16. Berlin: Evangelische Verlagsanstalt, 1988.

1094 Harold W. Attridge, *The Epistle to the Hebrews: A Commentary on the Epistle to the Hebrews*. Hermeneia Series. Philadelphia: Fortress Press, 1989.

1095 Claus P. März, *Hebräerbrief*. Würzburg: Echter Verlag, 1989.

1096 Erich Grässer, *An die Hebräer*. Zürich: Benziger Verlag, 1990.

1097 Susanne Lehne, *The New Covenant in Hebrews*. Sheffield: JSOT Press, 1990.

1098 Paul Ellingworth, *The Epistle to the Hebrews*. Epworth Commentary Series. London: Epworth Press, 1991.

1099 William L. Lane, *Hebrews*. Dallas: Word Books, 1991.

1100 *The Navarre Bible: The Epistle to the Hebrews in the Revised Standard Version and New Vulgate with a Commentary by Members of the Faculty of Theology of the University of Navarre*. Trans. Michael Adams. Dublin: Four Courts, 1991.

1101 August Strobel, *Der Brief an die Hebräer*.

1102 H.-F. Weiss, *Der Brief an die Hebräer: übersetzt und erklärt*. Göttingen: Vandenhoeck & Ruprecht, 1991.

1103 Ray C. Stedman, *Hebrews*. Downers Grove IL: InterVarsity Press, 1992.

1104 Paul Bernier, *A Key to the Letter to the Hebrews*. Ed. Herman Hendrickx. Quezon City, Philippines: Maryhill School of Theology, 1993.

1105 Paul Ellingworth, *The Epistle to the Hebrews: A Commentary on the Greek Text*. Grand Rapids: Eerdmans, 1993.

1106 Frances T. Gench, *Hebrews and James*. Louisville KY: Westminster John Knox Press, 1996.

1107 Charles R. Hume, *Reading through Hebrews*. London: SCM Press, 1997.

1108 T. G. Long, *Hebrews*. Louisville KY: John Knox Press, 1997.

1109 Victor C. Pfitzner, *Hebrews*. Nashville TN: Abingdon Press, 1997.

1110   George H. Guthrie, *Hebrews*. Grand Rapids: Zondervan, 1998.

Index